Total Physical Response©
in
FIRST YEAR SPANISH

Total Physical Response Activities for Beginning Spanish Students

by

Francisco Cabello, Ph.D.
Concordia College
Moorhead, Minnesota

edited by

James J. Asher, Ph.D.
Originator of the Total Physical Response,
known worldwide as TPR

illustrations by
Barbara Stewards

ISBN: 978-1-56018-499-7

published by

Sky Oaks Productions, Inc.
P.O. Box 1102 • Los Gatos, CA 95031

Phone: (408) 395-7600 • Fax: (408) 395-8440
e-mail: tprworld@aol.com • web: www.tpr-world.com

Free TPR Catalog upon request!

Copyright © 1985, 2007 • All Rights Reserved Worldwide.

All rights reserved under International and Pan-American copyright conventions. No part of this publication may be reproduced, stored in a retrieval system or transmitted in any form or by any means, electronic, mechanical, photocopies, recording or otherwise, without the prior written consent of the publisher.

Dr. Francisco L. Cabello is a native of Seville, Spain where he attended the University of Seville. He holds a B.A. in Modern Philology from the University of Seville, a Master's degree in English from Claremont Graduate University, and was awarded his Ph.D. in Spanish from the University of California at Davis. In his long teaching career, he has taught both Spanish and English.

His elementary and secondary language teaching experience includes the Foothill Country Day School (Claremont, California), Sacramento Country Day School (Sacramento, California), Colegio Público San José (La Puebla de Cazalla, Sevilla, Spain), and Canadian Language Institute (Montequinto, Seville, Spain).

He has taught at the following American colleges and universities: Pomona College (Claremont, California), University of California at Davis, Austin College (Sherman, Texas), Humboldt State University (Arcata, California), and Southern Oregon University (Ashland, Oregon), where he taught Spanish language, linguistics, translation, and methodology. Currently Dr. Cabello is Professor of Spanish at Concordia College in Moorhead, Minnesota.

Dr. Cabello is the author of the popular books **Total Physical Response in First Year Spanish, Total Physical Response in First Year English**, and **Total Physical Response in First Year French**. He has written the Spanish translations for all of James J. Asher's **TPR Student Kits**. He also co-authored the student workbook **Escuche y Actúe** (**Listen and Perform in Spanish**) with Stephen Mark Silvers. In 2001, in conjunction with the European Year of Languages he recorded a video, "Introduction to Total Physical Response" that was published in the CD-ROM **Lingua Snacks** (Teaching Language Taster Courses with Total Physical Response). To download articles he has written, go to www.tpr-world.com and then click on TPR Articles. You will enjoy his articles: *The ABCs of the Total Physical Response* and *A Simplified Guide to TPR Storytelling*.

Dr. Cabello was a featured speaker at the TPR international workshop *Motivating Children and Adults to Acquire Another Language*, presented in Los Gatos, California and at the University of Victoria, British Columbia, Canada.

He can be reached at the Department of Spanish and Hispanic Studies, Concordia College, 901 8th St. S. Moorhead, MN 56562-0001. His phone number: (218) 299-3103. E-mail: flcabello53@hotmail.com He welcomes your comments, suggestions, and questions.

Preface

Through the years, as I successfully applied the content of James J. Asher's now classic book *Learning Another Language through Actions* with my high school and college students, I discovered innovations that accelerated student involvement and excitement. I am pleased to share my experience with you in *Total Physical Response in First Year Spanish*. Your colleagues will enjoy my new books *Total Physical Response in First Year French* and *Total Physical Response in First Year English*.

For a sophisticated understanding of the stress-free Total Physical Response approach to second language learning, I recommend that you read *Learning Another Language Through Actions* by the originator of TPR, Dr. James J. Asher. Then follow-up with a fine book by Ramiro Garcia entitled *Instructor's Notebook: How To Apply TPR For Best Results*.

Francisco L. Cabello

Introduction

Use the lessons in this book as a dramatic script in which you are the director of the play and your students are the actors. The important difference between your production and a stage play is that you are the only one who has read the script.

You will be uttering directions in the target language and acting with the students for the first part of the lesson so that they instantly understand the meaning of what you are saying. I will guide you step by step in how to do this.

Later in Act 2 of the play, students will be ready to reverse roles with you and utter directions in Spanish to produce actions from you and other students in the class. As you move from lesson to lesson, I will cue you when it is time for role reversal. Notice that I use capital letters to let you know that you are talking to different students.

You will be amazed with the ease that your students understand what you are saying in Spanish. This is a heady experience for instructors and often encourages an ambitious attempt to race ahead. Resist the temptation! Relax. Take your time. Enjoy the experience along with your students.

Remember to introduce only three lexical items at a time. Do not proceed with new ones until students are responding with confidence to the previous set of three.

About Exhibits

In the first act of the play, students should not see any of the directions you are uttering in Spanish. As you make a smooth transition from lesson to lesson, I will cue you when to show students the directions in print.

Props and TPR Student Kits

You will need a variety of props for certain classes. In those cases I have listed, at the beginning of the lesson what you will need to have on hand that day. Also, certain lessons call for the additional use of James J. Asher's TPR Student Kits available from Sky Oaks Productions, Inc. Faced with the practical reality of not being able to take the students to, say, an actual home or supermarket, the instructor can always have the students use these kits to practice the intended lexical items and structures. Without leaving the classroom, my students use the TPR Student Kits to experience the target language in many different environments such as the home, kitchen, town, supermarket, restaurant, beach, gas station, farm, etc.

As you direct your students in the target language, they are making a physical response by placing a person or object in different locations on a playboard. For example, you may say in Spanish, *"Put the boy on the chair in his bedroom,"* and your students respond by placing the boy in his bedroom on the chair. The physical movement that each student makes when placing the figure of the boy is a *critical component* of TPR because it connects the words you just uttered in Spanish directly *through the physical response,* to each student's right brain. This makes for instant understanding at a *"deep level,"* to use Noam Chomsky's linguistic model. (To order TPR Kits online, go to www.tpr-world.com)

Reviews

Besides the specified review sessions, it is always a good idea to start every class with a review of the previous lesson as a warm up before introducing new material.

After listening comprehension, then what?

As you move step by step through this book, you will be delighted that your students understand everything you are saying in the target language. You will be surprised that they are internalizing Spanish rapidly in chunks rather than word by word.

As understanding of the spoken language expands and expands, your students will be reading without being aware that they are reading. The magic of TPR is that when the target language is internalized through body movements, students not only comprehend what you are saying but they comprehend what they see in print. This positive transfer from listening comprehension to reading is a huge saving in instructional time. Throughout this book, I guide your students into a smooth transition from listening fluency to reading without awareness.

The secret of "reading without awareness" is not to mention that the students are reading. They glide into "reading" by seeing messages in print and understanding what it says. For example, each student reaches into a hat, selects a strip of paper on which I have written ten commands in Spanish. My directions are: "Look at the paper and do what it says to do." I do not mention the word "reading." There is no such thing as "reading." There is only looking at symbols on paper and doing what it says to do.

How about speaking?

After about ten to twenty hours of understanding Spanish through physical movements, students spontaneously begin to speak in Spanish. Speaking cannot be forced, but will appear naturally as a playful activity. And when speaking appears, it will not be perfect. There will be many errors. But if we are as tolerant of student errors as we are of infants acquiring their first language, gradually speech will shape itself in the direction of the native speaker.

Throughout my book, I will help your students shape their speaking skills with role reversals, scenarios in which students play different parts, and skits that students create, stage, and act out.

How about writing?

As your students evolve from lesson to lesson, they will be writing without knowing that they are writing. In other words, we do not announce that, "Now you will be writing!" because this triggers resistance from the left brain which whispers sabotaging messages to the student such as, "Oh oh, this is something new! This will probably be difficult. You don't know how to write in Spanish. You will have trouble with this!" For a more sophisticated understanding of the right and left brain, see the back pages for a description of James J. Asher's book, *Brainswitching*. Also you will find a description of his latest book in which he has reinvented school using advanced research about how the left and right brain works. The title is, *The Super School of the 21st Century.*

Testing listening comprehension

In the final pages of this book you will find quizzes and tests that cover a vast amount of material. You may wish to create additional tests that are customized to your particular course objectives. I recommend that tests be taken as no more than a graded class session.

Here's how the testing works so that the experience not only demonstrates competency, but is enjoyable for both the students and the instructor: I put several versions of each quiz on strips of paper which I place in a hat. Then three or four students come into the room and each gets to reach in the hat for a slip of paper. Students enjoy having some control over the testing process.

Each student hands their strip of paper to me. I then read the commands and record the accuracy of each student's performance. I note on the paper any mistakes that have been made, and grade it with points decided in advance. This saves time because the quiz is graded immediately before the student leaves the room. Another powerful advantage of this procedure is that each student gets immediate feedback. You will be surprised how few mistakes are made!

Testing reading comprehension

For directions on when and how, to introduce reading, see Class 10. The testing is conducted just as we did for listening comprehension. That is, three or four students come into the room, select a slip of paper from the hat, look at what is written, and follow each direction on the paper. The instructor has the identical directions, and will be noting errors, if any, on the exam sheet.

Testing the entire class as a group

Realizing that many teachers have limited time for testing, Quiz 3, Quiz 4, and the Midterm Exam are designed to be given to the entire class as a single group. In Quiz 3 and Quiz 4, students are asked to write down either the information requested or an English translation of the Spanish commands.

Your students are on their way to fluency, now what?

You have enjoyed a successful experience with your students using Total Physical Response in First Year Spanish. How do you follow that act? I have discovered an exciting way that my students can continue to develop the three skills of speaking, reading, and writing.

NEW DEVELOPMENTS

Since the first edition of this book, there have been some exciting breakthroughs in stress-free acquisition of multiple languages. With the Total Physical Response as a foundation, there is another effective tool for making a smooth transition from understanding other languages in the first exposure with TPR to speaking, reading, and writing. That tool is TPR Storytelling by Blaine Ray and Todd McKay. You can order their books from the ads at the back of this book.

As you work with classic TPR, you will discover that your students have instant understanding of everything you are saying in the target language. As a result, students of all ages experience remarkable self-confidence as revealed in comments such as: "I can do this! I was afraid that I would not understand, but I get it. I am actually enjoying this language class!" For more helpful tips, go to www.tpr-world.com and then click on TPR Articles.

Once your students have internalized a batch of vocabulary and grammar in the target language with TPR, those items can be used to tell them a very short story. Follow up by coaching them to try telling the story to a classmate. Gestures are used to prompt the student step by step. As one young instructor told me recently on the telephone, "I was an average teacher, but these techniques of TPR followed by storytelling made me an outstanding instructor because my students are achieving fluency—not just ten percent of the class who will achieve no matter what the instructional strategy is—but 95 percent. It is extraordinary."

A personal invitation from Dr. Cabello...

As you apply TPR, you and your students will light up with exciting new ideas. You can look forward to being entertained by the novelty of the skits and stories your students create. If you have any questions or comments, please contact me by e-mail at flcabello53@hotmail.com Good luck! You are on the right track.

Table of Contents

About the Author

Preface

Introduction

Class One 1
Seating Arrangement, Introduction, Expansion of Utterances, Novelty, Keeping Your Promise, Introduction of New Vocabulary.

Class Two 5
Seating Arrangement, Review, New Commands, Expansion, Novel Commands, The Classroom.

Class Three 8
Props, Classroom Setup, New Commands, Parts of the Body, Review of New Material, A Final Note on Novelty.

Class Four 11
Props, Classroom Setup, Review, New Commands, Review, Draw a Face.

Class Five 15
Props, New Commands, Review, Role Reversal, Quiz 1: Classes 1-5, Reading, Exhibit 1.

Class Six 20
Props, Review, Novelty.

Class Seven 23
Props, Review, New Vocabulary Items, Questions "¿Dónde...?", Role Reversal, Reading and Writing

Class Eight 27
Props, Review, New Commands, Other Vocabulary, Manipulation of Numbers.

Class Nine 31
Props, Contrasts, Role Reversal

Class Ten 35
Props, Classroom Setup.

Class Eleven 39
Props, Classroom Setup, New Commands, More on Present Indicative, Introduction of "¿Quién...? ¿A quién...? ¿De quién...?", Reading: Exhibit 2.

Class Twelve 43
Props, Setup, Introduction of the Construction "¿Dónde está...?", More Practice With the Present Indicative, The Clothing Store Experience, A Video Presentation of a Clothing Store, Practice With Personal Data, Introduction of the Possessive Adjectives.

Class Thirteen 47
Props, Review of the Present Indicative, Review of the Clothing Store Experience, Reading: Exhibit 3, Quiz 2: Classes 6 - 13.

Class Fourteen 51
Props, Classroom Setup, Demonstrating the Present Indicative with Other Personal Pronouns such as: "Nosotros (-as), ustedes, ellos (as)," Introduction of the Days of the Week, Introduction of the Months of the Year, Crystal Ball Dates, More with the Question Word "quién."

Class Fifteen 55
Props, Continued Practice Manipulating Days of the Week, More Practice with the Months of the Year, New Commands, Review of the Present Indicative with "yo, tú, él, ella, nosotros (-as), ustedes, ellos (-as), More on Possessive Adjectives, Reading Stories: Story 1.

Class Sixteen 59
Props, Review of the Present Indicative, Review Contrasts Through Commands, Review Contrasts Through Short Answers, Then Into "yes" or "no" Answers, New Contrasts, Emotional or Affective States of Being, Play Statue, General Review.

Class Seventeen 65
Props, New Commands, Introduction of "saber."

Class Eighteen 69
Props, Review, Role Reversal, Pancho Carrancho.

Class Nineteen 71
Props, Classroom Setup, Reading Stories: Story 2, Review, Review of Question Words "qué," quién," "dónde," Review of the Days of the Week, Reading: Exhibit 4, Midterm Exam: Classes 1 - 19.

Class Twenty 75
Props, Review, New Material: The Preterite Tense, New Material: Occupational Vocabulary Items.

Class Twenty-One 77
Props, More with the Preterite Tense, More on Occupations, Reading and Writing: Exhibit 5.

Class Twenty-Two 79
Props, Review of Occupations, Reading: Exhibit 6.

Class Twenty-Three 81
Props, Classroom Setup, Review of the Preterite Tense, Introduction of Negation Combined with the Preterite Tense, Reading and Writing Personal Information: Exhibit 7.

Class Twenty-Four 83
Props, Review of Occupations, Continue with the Preterite Tense Requiring Short Answer Responses "sí/no," Reading: Exhibit 8, Telling Time, Continue with Time, Introduction of Fine Detail in Telling Time, More with the Preterite Tense, Writing: Exhibit 9, Pancho Carrancho with the Preterite Tense.

Class Twenty-Five 87
Props, Consumer Behavior, Contrast "este / ese / aquel," A Video of a Supermarket, More Food Vocabulary, Role Playing.

Class Twenty-Six 91
Props, Visit to a Local Supermarket, TPR Student Kit: The Supermarket©, Reading: Exhibit 10 (El Supermercado©).

Class Twenty-Seven 93
Props, Introduction of Places, Review of the Preterite Tense with Places, Introduction of the Preterite of "estar," Reading, Reading Sentences Created by the Students, Pancho Carrancho with the Preterite Tense and Vegetables.

Class Twenty-Eight 97
Props, Review of Constructed Sentences, Review of the Present Indicative and the Preterite Tense of the Verbs "ir," "ser," and "estar," More with Place Cards, Practice with Ordinal Numbers, Reading: Exhibit 11 (El Pretérito), Review of the Preterite, More with the Demonstrative Pronouns.

Class Twenty-Nine 101
Props, Classroom Setup, Review of the verb "estar," Pancho Carrancho with Place Cards, Creating a Story with a Place Card, Reading: Exhibit 12 (La Ciudad).

Class Thirty 103
Props, Classroom Setup, Introduction of Restaurant Vocabulary, Role Playing: A Fast Food Establishment.

Class Thirty-One 105
Props, Classroom Setup, More Restaurant Role Playing, Role Play Restaurant Situations, Ordinal Numbers, Everyday Dialogues, Practice with the Relative Clause.

Class Thirty-Two 109
Review of Everyday Dialogues: Exhibit 13 (Charla), Quiz 3: Classes 20 -32.

Class Thirty-Three 111
Props, Travelogue, Some Follow-up Geography, Object Description.

Class Thirty-Four 115
Props, Flags, Reading: Exhibit 14 (Viajes), Exhibit 15: Geografía, Family Vocabulary, Family Tree.

Class Thirty-Five 119
Props, Classroom Setup, Family Vocabulary, A Class Wedding, Introduction of Future Constructions, Future Imbedded in the Conditional.

Class Thirty-Six 121
Props, Classroom Setup, Review of Family Vocabulary: Exhibit 16 (La Familia), New Commands: the Home, TPR Student Kits: The Home©, The Kitchen©, The Toy House.

Class Thirty-Seven 123
Props, Review of Future Construction, More Practice with the Future Construction: Pancho Carrancho with Verb Cards, Future with Place Cards.

Class Thirty-Eight 125
Props, Role Reversal, Reviewing: Exhibit 17 (La Casa).

Class Thirty-Nine 127
Props, Costumes, Clothes Review, Home Review, Introduction of "hay," Describe Yourself: Adjectives.

Class Forty 131
Props, Classroom Setup, Review of "hay," Reviewing: Exhibit 18 (El Futuro Inmediato, Estructura "hay"), Review of "poder," more with Opposites.

Class Forty-One 135
Props, Review of Opposites: Exhibit 19 (Review of Constrasts, Introduction of "No puedo... porque...," An imaginary Car, Role Play a Gas Station Transaction, Reading: Exhibit 20 (El Coche), TPR Student Kit: the Gas Station©.

Class Forty-Two 139
Props, Classroom Setup, Situation 1: Al volante, Situation 2: En la cocina, Situation 3: En el banco, Situation 4: De compras, Situation 5: En el autobús, Quiz 4: Classes 33 - 42, Final Exam: Skits.

Tests 142
Quiz 1, Quiz 2, Midterm Exam, Quiz 3, Quiz 4, Final Exam: Skits.

A personal note from Francisco Cabello...
   The TPR approach electrifies my language classes with laughter, learning, and spontaneous interaction.
   To order the same TPR Student Kits, books and games that I use, call, fax, or write:

Sky Oaks Productions, Inc.
P.O. 1102, Los Gatos, CA 95031
Ph: (408) 395-7600 • Fax: (408) 395-8440
Ask for your free TPR Catalog!

CLASSROOM LESSONS

Class One

Seating Arrangement

Students should be sitting to the left and the right of the classroom, leaving a center isle to ensure walking space in the middle.

Introduction

If there is a common language to all students in your classroom and you know that language, prepare the students for the TPR approach by repeating Asher's opening recommendation in a casual and relaxed manner that inspires confidence and trust:

"Students, you are about to learn a new language in a very delightful way. When I say something in the new language, I will perform an action and you will do exactly what I do. Do not try to speak. Do not try to translate. Simply listen to what I say and do what I do. No work is necessary. I repeat: no work is necessary! Just listen—and trust that your body will know what to do." *Remember:*

- ✓ Do not repeat.
- ✓ Do not translate.
- ✓ Do not write anything down unless I tell you to.
- ✓ Just do what I ask you to do.

Tell the students that you are going to read ten commands, and that, by the end of the class, they will understand perfectly what these words mean. By doing this their attention is assured since they do not believe they can accomplish this in just one class.

Read the ten commands as quickly as you can, causing the reaction: "There is no way in the world I am going to understand what all that means." Reading fast will confirm their disbelief.

Levántense, Siéntense, Caminen, Párense, Den la vuelta, Salten, Señalen la puerta, Señalen la silla, Toquen la mesa, Toquen la ventana.

Ask for three or four volunteers. Before they have a chance to think about it, quickly pick them yourself, and ask them to come to the front of the classroom. Since no one person is all alone in front, students usually enjoy taking part in this "experiment."

Place five chairs in a row at the front of the class. Have the students sit on them. You take the one in the middle. Utter the following commands, perform them yourself, and indicate with gestures to the students to do what you are doing at the moment:

—¡Levántense!

—¡Siéntense!

Repeat these first two several times. Then do the following:

—Caminen.	—Den la vuelta.
—Párense.	—Caminen.
—Den la vuelta.	—Párense.
—Caminen.	—Salten.
—Párense.	—Den la vuelta.
—Salten.	—Siéntense.

At the end of the exercise, students and the instructor should be sitting where they were at the beginning.

Expansion of Utterances

Show the students as you utter the commands the first time, and have them do it too.
>—Señalen la puerta.
>—Señalen la silla.
>—Señalen la mesa.
>—Señalen la puerta.
>—Caminen a la puerta.
>—Toquen la puerta.
>—Señalen la silla. Caminen a la silla.
>—Toquen la silla.
>—Señalen la mesa. Caminen a la mesa. Toquen la mesa.

Let the students do it themselves without you showing them, since by now they should be confident.
>—Señalen una silla.
>—Caminen a una silla.
>—Siéntense.

*The instructor also sits down and direct **individual** students with commands such as:*
>—María, **levántese.**
>—José, **camine a la mesa.**
>—Carmen, **señale la puerta.**
>—Juan, **camine a la puerta y toque la puerta.**

Novelty

>—Luke, **señale una silla.**
>—Luke, **salte a la silla.**

If the student doesn't do it, you demonstrate by uttering:
>—Luke, **salte a la mesa.**

You jump toward the table, and then return to the student with:
>—Luke, **salte a la silla.**

To a student in the audience:
>—Jo Ann, **levántese.**
>—**Camine a la ventana.**
>—**Señale la mesa.**
>—**Toque la mesa.**
>—**Señale la silla.**
>—**Camine a la silla y siéntese.**
>—**Levántese.**
>—**Camine a la mesa.**
>—**Ahora siéntese en la mesa.**

Only if he/she doesn't, say the following, and demonstrate:
 —Jo Ann, **camine a la mesa.**

You walk to the table.
  —**Siéntese en la mesa.**

And you sit on the table, or:
  —María, **siéntese en la silla.**
  —**Levántese.**
  —**Siéntese en la silla.**
  —**Levántese y camine a la mesa.**
  —**Siéntese en la mesa.**

Keeping Your Promise

It is now time to test the students who volunteered. You will show them, and the whole class, that they now understand the ten commands which you rattled off at the beginning of the class. Once they successfully pass the test, ask other two or three students from the audience to do the same ten commands to show them that, even if they were not performing the actions themselves, they were still learning while listening to you, and watching other students moving around the classroom.

Introduction of New Vocabulary

Introduce these new items in commands, using them with the verbs already introduced.
  la luz
  la papelera
  la pared
  la pizarra
  el reloj
  el suelo
  el techo
  la ventana

Class Two

Props

pencils
paper
books

Seating Arrangement

Students should sit in a semicircle around the teacher's desk, so they can see well the action that is going to take place in this class.

Review

Select a small group from the audience, and move the students beginning with

—**Levántense.**

—**Siéntense.**

—**Levántense.**

—**Caminen.**

—**Párense.**

—**Den la vuelta.**

—**Salten.**

—**Siéntense.**

Then expand to

—**Caminen a la ventana.**

—**Toquen la ventana.**

—**Caminen a la mesa.**

—**Toquen la mesa.**

—**Caminen a la puerta.**

—**Toquen la puerta.**

—**Caminen a la silla.**

—**Toquen la silla.**

Call on individual students selected at random:

—(A), **levántate y camina a la mesa.**

—(B), **levántate y camina a la ventana.**

—(C), **camina a la mesa y siéntante en la mesa.**

New Commands

—(A), **levántate y camina a la mesa.**

When he/she responds, lead he student around the table so that both of you stand behind it, facing the class. All the items mentioned in this section should be on the table.

—**Toca el lápiz.**

The instructor and the student touch the pencil.
    —**Coge el lápiz.**

The instructor picks up the pencil and gestures for the student to pick up another pencil.
    —**Deja el lápiz sobre la mesa.**

Both put down their pencils.
    —**Toca el libro.**

Both touch the book.
    —**Coge el libro.**

Both pick up the book.
    —**Deja el libro sobre la mesa.**

The instructor delays response to see if assimilation is occurring.
    —**Toca el papel.**

Delay response to see if the student performs the correct action.
    —**Coge el papel.**

Delay response.
    —**Deja el papel sobre la mesa.**

Call two other students to the table. Move them through the usual routine:
    —**Levántense.**
    —**Caminen a la mesa.**

There should be enough pieces of paper, pencils, and books on the table for everyone to manipulate their own.
    —**Toquen el libro.**
    —**Toquen el papel.**
    —**Toquen el lápiz.**
    —**Cojan el libro.**
    —**Cojan el papel.**
    —**Cojan el lápiz.**
    —**Dejen el papel en la mesa.**
    —**Dejen el libro en la mesa.**
    —**Dejen el lápiz en la mesa.**
    —**Cojan el papel y el lápiz.**
    —**Dejen solamente el papel sobre la mesa.**
    —**Ahora dejen el lápiz sobre la mesa.**
    —**Cojan el lápiz y el libro.**
    —**Dejen el libro sobre la mesa, pero no dejen el lápiz sobre la mesa.**
    —**Cojan el papel.**
    —***No* dejen el papel sobre la mesa.**
    —***Ahora* dejen el papel sobre la mesa.**

Expansion

Move the students rapidly with the routine which is expanded to include:
    —**Abran el libro.**

Do it with the students the first time.
    —**Cierren el libro.**

The instructor closes the book, and the students close their books.

Novel Commands

Tell everybody to sit down with the familiar routine. Call on someone else with the familiar routine.
    —**(A), levántate. Camina a la mesa. Coge el lápiz y el papel.**

Wait and see how he/she does.
—Camina a la ventana y deja el lápiz sobre el suelo.

Wait and see how he/she does before you show him/her.
—Deja el papel en la silla.

Send the student to his/her chair with the familiar routine. Put a pencil on Student A's chair, and call on someone else.
—(B), levántate. Coge el lápiz de la silla de (A), y deja el lápiz sobre la mesa.
—(C), coge el libro y déjalo en la silla de (E).
—(E), coge el libro y ponlo en (F).
—(F), coge el libro y ábrelo.

—Cierra el libro y déjalo en la ventana.
—Coge el libro y déjalo en el suelo.
—Siéntate en el libro.
—Coge la silla y déjala en el suelo.

Finish the classroom introducing some of the items included in the following list that have not been taught yet. Use it as a reference.

La sala de clase

1. la estudiante
2. el profesor
3. el estudiante
4. el suelo
5. el techo
6. el libro
7. la ventana
8. el cristal
9. la tiza
10. la lámpara
11. la luz
12. el interruptor
13. la papelera
14. el enchufe
15. la silla
16. la pizarra
17. la mesa
18. la puerta
19. la pared
20. el borrador
21. el papel
22. el lápiz / la pluma

Class Three

Props

flash cards with numbers 1 - 10
book
pencil
dolls
skeleton (cardboard)

Setup

Display flash cards with numbers 1 - 10 on the board. Hang skeleton from board.

New Commands

Introduce the following lexical items by saying the following, and then doing it on the board:

nombre
> Voy a escribir mi nombre en la pizarra.
> Escribe tu nombre en la pizarra.
> (A), corre a la pizarra y escribe tu nombre.
> (B), ve a la pizarra y escribe tu nombre.
> Todos escriban su nombre en un papel.

dirección
> Voy a escribir mi dirección en la pizarra.
> Escribe tu nombre en la pizarra.
> (C), escribe tu nombre y dirección en la pizarra.
> Todos, escriban su dirección en un papel.

en / sobre
> (D), coge el libro,

Both the instructor and Student D pick up a book.

> y ponlo en la silla.

They put their books on the chair.

> Pon el libro en la mesa.
> Ponte el libro en la cabeza.
> Deja el libro sobre la mesa.

Demonstrate.

debajo de
> (E), coge el lápiz,

Both the instructor and Student E pick up a pencil.

> y ponlo debajo de la silla.

They put their pencils under a chair.
>(F), coge tu lápiz y ponlo debajo de la mesa. (PAUSE.)
>Ahora, pon el lápiz debajo del libro.

números del 1 al 10.
>Voy a escribir el número 1 en la pizarra.
>Voy a escribir el número 2.
>Voy a escribir el 3.

This continues through number 10.
>(A), escribe los números 1 y 2 en la pizarra.
>(B), escribe el 3.
>(C), escribe el 4 y el 5.

Parts of the Body

cabeza
>(A), tócate la cabeza.

Touch your head while Student A touches his/hers.
>Todos, tóquense la cabeza.
>(B), tócale la cabeza a (C).

boca
>(A), tócate la boca.

And the instructor touches his/her mouth while Student A touches hi/hers.
>Todos, tóquense la boca.
>(B), tócate la cabeza. Tócate la boca.

oreja (s)
>(A), tócate las orejas.

The instructor touches his/her ears while Student A touches his/hers.
>(B), tócate una oreja.
>Ahora tócate las dos orejas.
>(C), tócale las orejas a (D).

ojo (s)
>(A), tócate los ojos.

The instructor touches his/her eyes while Student A touches his or hers.
>Todos, tóquense los ojos.
>(B), tócate un ojo.
>Ahora, tócate los dos.

mano (s)
>Voy a tocarle las manos a (C).
>(B), tócame las manos.
>(C), tócame una mano.
>(D), pon una mano en la mesa.
>(E), ponle las manos en la cabeza a (F).

brazo (s)
    Voy a tocarle el brazo a (A).
    Voy a tocarle los brazos a (B).
    (C), **tócale los dos brazos a** (D).
    (E), **tócame un brazo.**

pierna (s)
    Voy a tocarme las piernas.
    Voy a tocarme una pierna.
    (A), **tócate las piernas.**
    Todos, tóquense una pierna.
    Tóquense las dos piernas.

nariz
    Voy a tocarme la nariz.

And so on. Remember not to introduce too much new material at one time. Try working with only three new items. When students are responding confidently to those items, try three more, such as:

    dedo (s)
    pecho
    cara
    cuello

Partes del cuerpo

la cabeza	el cuello
el ojo	el (los) brazo (s)
la cara	la (s) mano (s)
la(s) oreja (s)	el (los) dedo (s)
la nariz	la (s) pierna (s)
la boca	el pecho

Review of New Material

Instructor utters one command at a time, then two in a row to move people all over the room.

A Final Note on Novelty

It is wise to write out the exact commands you will be using especially the novel ones because the action is so fast-moving, there is usually no time for you to think on your feet. Here are some examples. But if the context prompts you a new, original recombination that you don't have in your script, by all means, use it. Refer to the big flash cards with numbers printed on them.

    Coge el número 3 y el número 7, y ponte el 3 en la cabeza.
    Pon el número 10 debajo de la silla.
    Coge el libro, pon el número 5 en el libro, y ponte el libro debajo del brazo.
    Tócate la nariz con el lápiz.

Class Four

Props

paper (white paper, pink paper)
pencils
pens (blue pen, yellow pen)
books (red book, blue book)

flowers
magazines
flash cards with numbers 1 - 15
envelops with pieces of paper containing numbers 1 - 10

Classroom Setup

Display flash cards with numbers on board.

Review

A fast moving review with individuals, small groups and the entire class. Two, three and even four commands in rapid succession.

¡Levántate!
¡Salta!
¡Da la vuelta!
¡Coge la silla, y pon la silla en la mesa!

New commands

Verbs

golpear
- Golpéate el brazo.
- Golpea la mesa.
- Golpea a (A).
- Golpéame en la mano.
- Golpéame la cara.
- Golpéate el pecho.

Tirar
- Tira el papel al suelo.
- Tírame el lápiz.
- Tírale el libro a (A).

Dar
- Dame el libro.
- Dame el lápiz.
- Dale el papel a (B).

Tomar
- Toma el libro.
- Toma el lápiz.
- Toma el papel de (B).

Encender
- Enciende la luz.

Apagar
- Apaga la luz.

Nouns

flor (s)
- Coge la flor y ponla debajo del libro.
- Tírame la flor.
- Golpea a (A) con la flor.

revista (s)
- Dale la revista a (A).
- (B), coge la revista que tiene (A) y dámela.
- Pon la flor sobre la revista.
- Dale las revistas a (B).
- (B), pon las revistas en el suelo.
- Coge las revistas del suelo y dáselas a (A).

Tiza
- Camina a la pizarra, coge la tiza, y dásela a (B).
- (B), ponte la tiza en la cabeza.
- (C), toma la tiza de la cabeza de (B) y escribe tu nombre en la pizarra.

Pluma
- Coge la pluma de la mesa.
- Ponte la pluma en la oreja.

Colores
- (A), toca el libro rojo.
- Toca el libro azul.
- Coge la pluma azul y tírasela a (B).
- Dame el papel rosa y la pluma amarilla.

Números

Review

Distribute envelopes to students with pieces of papers with numbers 1 - 10 printed on them. Have students manipulate these with commands like

> Pon el 2 debajo del 7.
> Pon el 8 sobre el 10.

Numbers 11 - 15

Each number from 1 through 15 is on a large flash card which students manipulate.

  (A), **Coge el 11 y el 12 tíraselos a (B).**
  (C), **pon el 12 y el 15 en la silla.**
  (D), **señala el 14.**

Draw a face

Ask students to take out a piece of paper and draw a face as you say:

  Dibuja una cara.

Quickly continue with
  Dibuja los ojos.
  Dibuja las orejas.
  Dibuja la boca.
  Dibuja la nariz.

Class Five

Props

book
scissors
paper
a picture of a cat
watch
dolls (brunette, blonde)

Review

—(A), coge el libro de la mesa y pónselo en la nariz a (B).
—(B), tírame el libro, golpea a (A) en el brazo, y dibuja una cara feliz en la pizarra.

Draw the face yourself because "feliz" is introduced for the first time.

—(C), camina con (D) a la mesa. Ahora pon a (D) en la mesa.
—Dame tu reloj.
—Ponte el reloj en la oreja.
—Pon tu reloj debajo de tu silla.

New Commands

Dibujar
- Dibuja tu nombre en la pizarra. Dibuja un círculo alrededor de tu nombre.

Show the student by drawing a circle around his/her name.
- Dibuja una mesa en tu papel.
- Dibuja una cara feliz en la pizarra y escribe el nombre de (A) debajo.

Reírse de
- Señala en la pizarra la cara feliz que se ríe.
- (B), camina a la mesa y siéntate en la mesa.
- (A), ríete de (B), que está sentado en la mesa.
- (C), cuando diga tu nombre, ríete.

Look at the student, and say his/her name loud and clear.

Cortar
- Corta el papel que está sobre la mesa.

Show the student by cutting a piece of paper with your scissors.
- Dibuja un círculo en el papel.

Wait until he/she draws a circle.
- Corta el círculo que dibujaste en el papel.
- Dibuja una mesa en el papel.

Pause.
- Corta la mesa que dibujaste en el papel.
- Corta el papel por la mitad.

Show the student by cutting the paper in half.

As a rule, always demonstrate the first time a new lexical item is introduced, after uttering the command. Then repeat the same command, and wait for the student to perform the action.

Correr
- Corre a la ventana.
- Corre a la puerta.
- Corre a la pizarra.

Mostrar
- Muestra las manos.
- Muestra tu papel a (A).
- Muestra tu libro a (B).

Empujar
- Empuja la mesa.
- Empuja la silla.
- Empuja a (A) en su silla.

Tirar de

Before you give the command, put a chair under the table.
- Tira de la silla.
- Tira de la puerta.
- Tira de mi brazo.

Gritar
- Grita.
- Grita cuando mires la cara feliz que (B) dibujó en la pizarra.
- (A), golpea a (B) en el brazo. (B), grita cuando (A) te golpee en el brazo.
- (C), grita cuando yo te llame.

And call the student with an ominous voice.

The verbs are then combined with these lexical items:

línea recta
- Corre a la pizarra y dibuja una línea recta.
- Dibuja con el dedo una línea recta.
- (A), (B), y (C)—caminen a la pizarra en una línea recta.

línea curva
- (D), corre a la pizarra y dibuja una línea curva junto a la línea recta.
- (E), camina a la mesa en una línea curva.
- (F), dibuja con el dedo una línea curva.

círculo
- Dibuja un círculo.
- (A), escribe el número 13 en la pizarra y dibuja un círculo alrededor.
- (B), corre a la pizarra y dibuja un círculo. Después escribe tu nombre en el círculo.
- (D), dibuja un círculo en tu papel.

cuadrado
- Dibuja un cuadrado.
- (A), escribe el número 11 en la pizarra y después dibuja un cuadrado alrededor.
- (B), escribe tu nombre en la pizarra, y después dibuja un cuadrado alrededor.
- (C), en tu papel, dibuja un cuadrado. Dentro del cuadrado dibuja un círculo.

gato
- (A), coge el gato y dáselo a (B).
- (B), dale el gato a (C).
- (D), corre a la pizarra y dibuja un gato.

hombro (s)
- (A), tócale los hombros a (B). (PAUSE.) Golpéale en el hombro.

Pause.
- (B), grita.
- (C), tócate los hombros.

rodilla (s)
- Tócate las rodillas.
- Tócate las rodillas con un lápiz.
- Corre a la mesa y pon la rodilla sobre la mesa.
- Ponte las manos en las rodillas, y ríete.

pie (s)
- Tócate el pie.
- Tócate los pies.
- Ponte el libro en el pie.
- (A), deja caer la tiza sobre el pie de (B).
- (C), escribe en tu papel el número de pies que tiene (D).
- Golpea el suelo con el pie.

pelo

Touch your hair and say:
- (A), tócale el pelo a (B).

Go to a student with black hair and touch it while saying:
- Si tienen el pelo negro, levántense.

And motion these students to stand up.
- Siéntense.
- Si (B) tiene el pelo negro, ríanse de él.

Go to a student with blond hair, and do the same.
- Si tienen el pelo rubio, levántense. (PAUSE.) Siéntense.
- (C), si (D) tiene el pelo rubio, golpéala en el brazo.
- Tírate del pelo y grita.
- Si usted tiene el pelo negro, levántese por favor.

reloj
- Dame tu reloj.
- Ponte el reloj en la oreja.
- Pon tu reloj debajo de la silla.

entre
- Escribe los números 11 y 12 en la pizarra.

Pause.
- Dibuja una línea recta entre los números 11 y 12.

Ask two students, Student A and Student B sitting at different ends of the classroom to stand up. Then say:
- (C), camina entre (A) y (B).

Take a few steps away from your desk, and say:
- (D), pon la silla entre la mesa y yo.

junto a
- Dibuja un círculo en la pizarra.
- Escribe el número 15 junto al círculo.
- (A), ponte de pie junto a (B).
- (C), pon tu libro junto al hombro de (D).

alrededor de
- Escribe tu nombre en la pizarra.
- Dibuja un círculo alrededor de tu nombre.
- Camina alrededor de la mesa y grita.
- Con el dedo, dibuja un círculo alrededor de tu oreja.

Review

Review all items in Exhibit 1 orally.

Role Reversal

Invite the students to give you commands using the items introduced. They usually come up with surprisingly funny ones. No matter what they say, you should always do it, so that, when you ask them to do something out of the ordinary, they will not be shy or embarrased.

Quiz 1 (Classes 1 - 5)

See the section on **Tests** at the end of the book.

Reading

Distribute **Exhibit 1** which has all the vocabulary and grammatical structures which the students now understand when they are read by the instructor. Read each item and act it out. Students do not read aloud nor repeat each word or phrase.

Exhibit 1

VERBOS	LA SALA DE CLASE	ESTRUCTURAS
levántese	la mesa	1. Toque la mesa.
siéntese	la silla	2. Escriba su nombre.
camine	la ventana	3. Encienda la luz.
párese	la puerta	4. Coja la flor roja.
dé la vuelta; salte	la luz	5. Señale el suelo.
señale	el techo	6. Dibuje un círculo en la pizarra.
toque	el suelo	
coja	el reloj	
deje sobre / ponga en	la pared	una línea recta / curva
escriba	la pizarra	un círculo
abra	el papel	un cuadrado
corra	el gato	
cierre	el lápiz	LOS COLORES
golpee	la pluma	rojo (a)
tire	la papelera	verde
encienda	el libro	rosa
apague	el nombre	azul
dé	la tiza	amarillo (a)
tome	la revista	negro (a)
dibuje	la flor	blanco (a)
ríase (de)		rubio (a)
corte		
muestre		
empuje	EL CUERPO	PREPOSICIONES
tire de	la cabeza	sobre (en) / debajo de
grite	la boca	entre
	el ojo (s)	alrededor de
	la nariz	junto a
	la oreja (s)	con
	el pecho	
	el brazo (s)	LOS NUMEROS
	la pierna (s)	1 uno 9 nueve
	el hombro (s)	2 dos 10 diez
	la rodilla (s)	3 tres 11 once
	el pie (s)	4 cuatro 12 doce
	el pelo	5 cinco 13 trece
	la mano (s)	6 seis 14 catorce
	el dedo (s)	7 siete 15 quince
	la cara	8 ocho
	el cuello	

Class Six

Props

Many of these items can be made of plastic.

apple	glass
orange	banana
orange juice (empty carton)	3 pencils (one green)
apple juice (empty carton)	6 pieces of paper
pear	toy car
water (empty bottle)	spoon
milk (empty carton)	knife
coffee (empty can)	fork
cup	bread
	2 flowers (red, white)

Review

Fast moving review of previously introduced commands. Get students in motion performing different actions simultaneously.

New Commands

Display all those items listed under Props on your desk. Remember to demonstrate the actions, and to point out the new items to the students until they feel confident responding to them. Students do not actually need to eat or drink; simply mimicking the actions is enough to convey the meaning.

Come
- la naranja.
- la manzana.
- la pera.
- pan.
- la banana.

Echa
- agua en el vaso.
- café en la taza.
- leche en el vaso.

Levanta
- el vaso de la mesa.

Pretend you are proposing a toast as you demonstrate the command.
- Llévatelo a la boca.
- Bebe.
- Levanta la taza de la mesa.
- Levanta el brazo.
- Levanta la mano.

Bebe
- agua.
- leche.
- café.
- un poco de jugo de naranja.
- un poco de agua y dale el vaso a (A).

You can now recombine these new verbs and other familiar ones with the food items presented in this lesson.

Come
- la naranja.
- la manzana.
- la banana.
- pan.

Echa
- agua en el vaso.
- café en la taza.

Bebe
- leche.
- un poco de jugo de naranja.
- un poco de jugo de manzana.
- un poco de agua y dale la taza a (A)

Coge
- el tenedor y la cuchara.

Corta
- el pan con el cuchillo.
- la manzana.
- la naranaja.

Toca
- la naranja.
- la manzana.
- la banana.
- el pan.

Coge
- la naranja.
- la manzana.
- la banana.
- el pan.
- la taza de la mesa.
- el tenedor.
- el cuchillo.

Dame
- la naranja.
- la manzana.
- la banana.
- el pan.
- la taza.
- el tenedor.
- el cuchillo.

Echa
- agua en el vaso.
- café en la taza.
- leche en el vaso.
- un poco de agua en la ventana.

Coge
- el tenedor.
- la cuchara.
- el cuchillo y ponlo debajo de la silla de (B).
- el pan y cómetelo.
- un vaso de agua.

More New Commands

Cuenta
- tres lápices y dámelos.
- cinco estudiantes y tócales la cabeza.
- seis papeles en la mesa y dáselos a (B).

Conduce
- el coche a la pizarra.
- el coche alrededor de la silla.
- el coche a la silla de (A).

Pita
- Conduce el coche y pita.
- Pita tres veces.
- Conduce el coche y pita cuando pases delante de (B).

Novelty

Create novel, sometimes zany commands. These enliven the class, and you will find out that students can comprehend them perfectly. Here are some examples:

—(A), coge el tenedor, el cuchillo y la cuchara, y ponlos en tu silla.

The next three commands should be done as a sequence. Give a piece of bread to (A), and then say:

—(B), coge el pan de (A), golpéalo en el brazo, y cómete el pan.

—(A), coge un vaso de agua.

Pause.

—Echa un poco de agua en la cabeza de (B), y ríete.

—Ponte de pie en tu silla y salta.

—Coge la flor roja y el lápiz verde. Pon el lápiz en la taza y ponte la flor en la oreja.

Class Seven

Props

Toy car	toothbrush
book (red)	toothpaste
knife	clothesbrush
spoon	rectangle
cup	square
water	triangle
soap	hairbrush
flower (red)	shoebrush
towel	hair drier
comb	

Review

Fast moving warm-up in which individual students are moved with commands.

—(A), conduce el coche alrededor de (B) y pita.
—(C), tira la flor roja a (D).
—Grita.
—Coge el cuchillo y la chuchara y ponlos en la taza.
—(E), bebe un poco de agua y dale la taza a (F).

New Commands

Mime these new actions to convey their meaning to the students, and point out the new objects.

Láva(te)
- las manos.
- la cara.
- la cabeza.
- el pelo.
- la taza.

Sécate
- las manos.

Just for fun, use your sweater to dry your hands.
- la cara.
- la cabeza.
- el pelo.

Mimic as if you were using a hair drier.

Busca
- la toalla.
- el jabón.
- un peine.

Sostén
- el libro.
- la taza.
- el jabón.

Péina(te)
- el pelo.
- a (A).
- a (B).

Cepílla(te)
- los dientes.
- los pantalones.
- los zapatos.
- el pelo.
- la mesa.

New Vocabulary Items

rectángulo
- Dibuja un rectángulo en la pizarra.
- Coge un rectángulo de la mesa y dámelo.
- Pon el rectángulo junto al cuadrado.

triángulo
- Coge el triángulo de la mesa y dámelo.
- Coge el triángulo y ponlo junto al rectángulo.
- Coge el triángulo y el cuadrado y pónselos en la cabeza a (A).

rápidamente
Give these commands with a sense of urgency to make plain the meaning of the adverb.
- Camina rápidamente a la puerta y golpéala.
- Rápidamente, corre a la mesa y toca el cuadrado.
- Rápidamente siéntate y ríete.

lentamente
Pronounce the adverb very slowly.
- Camina lentamente a la ventana y salta.
- Lentamente, levántate.
- Camina lentamente hacia mí y golpéame en el brazo.

cepillo de dientes
- Saca tu cepillo de dientes.
- Cepíllate los dientes.
- Pon el cepillo de dientes en tu libro.

pasta de dientes
- Busca la pasta de dientes.
- Abre la pasta de dientes.
- Echa un poco de pasta de dientes en el cepillo.
- Ponle el tapón.
- Cepíllate los dientes.
- Tírale la pasta de dientes a (B).

dientes
- Tócate los dientes.
- (A), muestra los dientes a (B).
- (B), señálale los dientes a (A).

jabón
- (A), busca el jabón.
- Dale el jabón a (B).
- (A), ponle el jabón a (B) en la oreja.

toalla
- Ponle la toalla en el brazo (C).
- Ponte la toalla en la cabeza y ríete.
- Sécate las manos con la toalla.

Questions (¿Dónde ...?)

Students can answer by pointing. After all the previous sets of commands, the items mentioned in these questions will now be scattered around the classroom.

—¿Dónde está la toalla?
—¿Dónde está el cepillo de dientes?
—¿Dónde está (A)?

Role Reversal

Get volunteers to give commands to you or to other students.

Reading and Writing

Write on the board each new vocabulary item and a command to illustrate it. Then read each item and act out the commands. Students will listen as the instructor reads the material. It is up to individual students to decide whether or not they want to copy the information in their notebooks.

Class Eight

Props

paper
scissors
water
flash-cards with large numbers 1 - 25
cardboard triangle (to be cut)
cardboard rectangle (to be cut)
cardboard square (to be cut)
book

Review

Quick review to warm up.

Classroom Setup and Strategy

The second part of this class is very much about body functions, such as sleeping, waking up, snoring, etc. Select two or three students and have them sit on desks in front of the class. The whole class can also perform the actions. For sleeping, students can just lay their heads on their desks. Coordinate the sequence of commands in such a way as to illustrate the meaning of the command that follows. For example, when you tell the students to sleep, have them sleep continuously, so that, when you give them the next command (to wake up), the meaning is apparent. As always when introducing new lexical items, act them out yourself the first two or three times you use them, until students are responding confidently to them.

Also display at random the flash-cards numbered 1 - 25 on the board, 1 - 10 flat on the floor, and; 11 -25 upright against the blackboard.

New Commands

dormir
- Cierren los ojos y duérmanse.
- Cuando cuente "tres", duérmanse.

And count to three slowly but audibly.

roncar
- Cierren los ojos, duerman y ronquen.
- (A), ponte la cabeza en los brazos, duerme y ronca.
- ¿Roncó (A)?

Despertar
- (A) duerme. (B), despiértalo.
- Despierta, levántate y lávate la cara.
- Despierta y grita.
- Despierta y ríete.

Mover
- Despierta, levántate y mueve las manos.
- (A), mueve los pies.

Pellizcar
- Pellízcate el brazo.
- (A), pellízcale la nariz a (B).
- (C), golpéale el brazo a (D) y pellízcale la nariz.

Other Vocabulary

mano (s)
- Levanta las manos.
- Muéstrame las manos.

Por la mitad
- Corta el papel por la mitad.
- Corta el triángulo por la mitad.
- Corta el cuadrado por la mitad.

detrás de
- Ponte las manos detrás de la cabeza.
- Pon el papel detrás de _____.

Ask (A) to turn around, and, while s/he is not looking, hide a book behind (B). Then say:
- (A), busca el libro que está detrás de (B) y dámelo.
- Ponte las manos detrás de ti.

Ask three students, A, B, and C to stand up. Then make them line up behind you in that order.
- (D), pon a (A) detrás de (B).

Help Student D to motion the bodies if s/he is reluctant to do it. Afterwards, give commands to form every possible combination in the line-up. For example:
- Pon a (B) detrás de (C).
- Pon a (A) detrás de (B), y a (C) detrás de (A).

Hide flash-card number 17 behind your back. Then say:
- Rápidamente, busca el número 17 detrás de mí.

Delante de
- Rápidamente, pon el número 13 delante del 7.
- Pon a (A) delante de (B).
- Pon a (C) delante de (B).

Con
- (A), camina con (B) a la pizarra.
- (C), corre con (D) a la pizarra.
- (D), corre con (E) a la puerta y salta.
- Bebe café con leche.

Manipulation of Numbers

Flash cards with numbers 1 through 10 should be flat on the floor. Flash cards numbered 11 through 25 should be standing upright against the board, so that the meaning of prepositions detrás de and debajo de are evident later. Use the flash cards on the floor when prepostion debajo de is involved, and the ones on the board when detrás de is. Ask students to change the location of the flash cards to practice the numbers along with already familiar prepositions. Here are some examples. Expand until students respond without hesitation.

—Pon los números del 1 al 10 en una línea recta.

—Ahora pon el 1 debajo del 5.

—Pon el 10 detrás del 12.

—Pon el 21 delante del 24.

—Pon el 25 detrás del 23.

—Pon el 20 junto al 13.

—Pon el número 22 sobre el número 4.

Class Nine

Props

string (a long and a short piece)
pencils (a long and a short one)
colored pencils (1 yellow; use a can to hold them up)
picture of a sad face
picture of a happy face
knife
spoon
fork
2 cups (one white)
1 bottle of water (empty)
$5 bill
scarf (to cover eyes)
dance music on tape
song on tape ("Feliz cumpleaños" or any other popular tune)

Contrasts

Show the meaning of these opposite adjectives by pointing to the items the first time you use them in a command.

derecha / izquierda
- Levanta la mano derecha.
- Levanta la mano izquierda.
- Levanta el pie derecho.
- Levanta el pie izquierdo.
- Camina y da la vuelta a la derecha.
- Camina y da la vuelta a la izquierda.
- Levántate, camina a la ventana y da la vuelta a la derecha.

Cover someone's eyes with a scarf. Direct their movements around the room using 'izquierda' and 'derecha'. After a while, left the other students give the commands. You can begin someone near the blackboard. Move the student around the room using commands such "Da dos pasos adelante," "Da la vuelta a la derecha" etc. The student will finish next to the board.

Another action approach to learning directions is to line up a few students as a military formation. Ask students to march and direct them with instructions such as "Izquierda, derecha, izquierda."

largo / corto
- Ponte el lápiz largo en la mano derecha y el corto en la cabeza.

While the student is holding the two pencils, ask the class the following. They can answer by pointing:
- ¿Dónde está el lápiz largo?
- ¿Dónde está el lápiz corto?

Hold the long piece of string at one end, and have a student pull from the other. Then say:
- (A), tira de la cuerda larga.

Stretch the string as far as it can go. Then put it down, and repeat the operation with the short string.
- (B), tira de la cuerda corta.

feliz / triste

Invite two students to come to the front. Have the students hold the pictures or drawings of a sad face and a happy face. Point to the pictures when you give the commands. Call on some other student.

- _____, dale la mano al estudiante triste.
- Dale el lápiz amarillo al estudiante feliz.
- Ponte detrás del estudiante feliz.
- Dale 5 dólares al estudiante triste.

Pause. Pointing to the student with the five dollars, say:

- Este estudiante está feliz ahora.

And switch the pictures they were holding.

- Dile al estudiante triste que baile.

Dance yourself to show the meaning of the verb. Do the same with 'canta' and 'abraza' in the next two commands.

- Camina alrededor del estudiante triste y canta.
- Abraza al estudiante triste.

alto / bajo

Call a tall and a short student to the front of the class. Touch the tall student on the head, and say:

- (A) es alto (-a).

Then lower your hand to the short student's head, and say:

- (B) es bajo (-a).
- (A) es alto (-a) y (B) es bajo (-a).
- (C) ponte junto al estudiante alto.
- Siéntate delante del estudiante.
- Dale un cuchillo, una cuchara y un tenedor al estudiante bajo.

Now ask the class:

- ¿Cómo se llama el estudiante alto?

Pause.

- ¿Cómo se llama el estudiante bajo?

mojado / seco

Hand the student the empty bottle of water. The student will pretend to pour water.

- Echa agua en la taza blanca.
- Ahora, tira el agua a la ventana cerca de la mesa.

Pretend.

- Señala con el dedo la ventana **mojada.**
- Señala la ventana **seca.**
- Camina a la ventana **mojada** y tócala.
- Corre a la ventana **seca** y ábrela.
- (A), pon un poco de agua en la mano de (B).

Wait for Student A to do this.

- (C), corre rápidamente y tócale a (B) la mano mojada.
- Tócale la mano seca.

Role Reversal

Bring a visitor to class that knows Spanish or a more advanced student, and have the students give commands to him/her. They will be astonished to realize that they can manipulate other people's behavior in the language they are learning. If you can't find anyone, have your students give you commands.

Reading and Writing

Write the new items on the board: **baila, canta, abraza, cuerda**, etc. Pronounce each item and act them out, or show them.

Class Ten

Props

book	picture or drawing of an angry man
cup	picture or drawing of the same man smiling
paper	picture or drawing of the same man with a sad expression
spoon	
ball	picture or drawing of an angry woman
umbrella	picture or drawing of the same woman smiling
frisbee	picture or drawing of the same woman with a sad expression
ball	
flowers	

Class Setup

Display the pictures of the man and woman on the board.

Review

Fast moving. Students perform actions simultaneously.

New Material

Deja caer
- el libro en el suelo.
- la taza en la mesa.
- el papel en la cabeza de _____.

Coge
- (A), coge el libro que te voy a tirar.

And throw the book to the student.
- (B), Coge la cuchara que te voy a tirar.

And throw the spoon.
- (C), coge esta pelota.

And throw the ball.

Llora
- (A), golpea a (B).

A pause.
- (B), llora.
- Cuando te pellizque el brazo, llora.

Go to a student and pinch him/her on the arm.

Mira
- Mírame y llora.

Enfadado
- (A), golpéame en el brazo. Mira (A). Estoy enfadado.

And get angry.
- (B), cuando te golpee, enfádate.

And tap the student slighly on the arm.
hombre / mujer
- Coge la foto del hombre enfadado y dámela.

Sonríe

Pointing to the right pictures, say:
- **En esta foto la mujer sonríe.**
- En esta foto la mujer no sonríe.
- En esta foto el hombre sonríe.
- Rápidamente, (A), tira la mujer que sonríe a (B).
- (C), sonríe.
- Mírame y sonríe.
- Todos sonrían.

paraguas
- Coge el paraguas.
- (A), dale el paraguas a (B).
- (B), golopea a (C) con el paraguas.

pelota
- Coge la pelota.

Bota
- Bota la pelota dos veces.

Gesture to the student to bounce the ball.
- Tírale la pelota a _____ después de haberla botado cinco veces.

frisbee
- Tírame el frisbee.
- Coge el frisbee.

Use more objects. Get the ball and pose as a goalkeeper. Look straight ahead as you ask the students to throw you the object:
- Tírame la pelota.

Ask everyone to stand up. Then say:
Tírale el frisbee al hombre más alto de la clase.

Introduction of the Present Indicative

(e.g., yo / tú / él stem + -o, -as, -a / -o, -es, -e)

Notice how the grammatical feature is imbedded in the imperative. Whenever practicing the Present Indicative, hint to the students they should keep doing what you told them to do until you send them back to their seats, so that the meaning of the tense becomes clear when giving related commands or asking questions on the action they are performing.

—(A), toca la mesa.

A pause.

  —(B), toca la mesa que toca (A).
  —(C), toca la ventana.

A pause.

  —(D), toca la ventana que toca (C).
  —(E), lentamente, dibuja un cuadrado en la pizarra.

A pause.

  —(F), dibuja un círculo alrededor del cuadrado que dibuja (E).
  —(G), lentamente, escribe tu nombre en la pizarra.

A pause.

  —(H), borra el nombre que (G) escribe.

Practice of Numbers

Ask the students to pick up pencil and paper, and write the numbers as you say them:

  —Cojan papel y lápiz y escriban los números que les voy a decir.

After saying each number, give students a chance to write them down. Then write the number on the board for immediate feedback. Begin with regular intervals such as 10, 20, 30, 40 ..., 100, 200, 300 ..., and then irregular intervals such as 22, 138, 67, etc. If it looks to you as too many numbers for one day, do through one hundred today and the rest tomorrow, i.e. first day: 10 - 100; second day: 100 - 1,000.000

Role Reversal

Ask students to give you numbers in Spanish and you write them on the board.

Questions

These questions only require an answer of one or two words.

  —¿Cuántos dedos tienes?
  —_____, tócate la nariz.

A pause.

  —¿Cuántas narices tienes?
  —_____, cierra los ojos.

A pause.

  —¿Cuántos ojos tienes?
  —_____, tócate la cabeza.

A pause.

  —¿Cuántas cabezas tienes?

A pause.

  —Señálate los dientes.
  —¿Cuántos dientes tienes?

Give the flowers to a student.

  —_____, cuenta las flores.

A pause.

  —¿Cuántas flores tienes?

Transfer to Reading

Use a transparency on the overhead projector on which are printed in large characters the limited directions in Class One (i.e., levántate, siéntate, camina, párate, da la vuelta, etc.). Then invite a student to participate with, "Cuando yo te muestre algo en la pantalla, haz lo que pone la frase."

Cover the whole transparency with a piece of paper and start uncovering one command at a time. The student who volunteered will begin to perform the actions called for in the written commands. There will be a graceful transition from comprehension to reading if you are casual. Avoid using the word 'reading'. That is, it is important not to announce to the students that they will be reading. Simply present the exercise the way shown above, and start.

Class Eleven

Props

hangers	dress	signs for 'fitting room'
jacket	spoon	piece of paper with something written on it
sweater	book	
blouse	pants	all items and pictures for Exhibit 2
shirt	*(large enough to wear over student's own)*	
skirt		
raincoat		

Classroom Setup

Try to recreate the atmosphere of a department store by displaying clothing items hanging on hangers or on tables and chairs. Extra large sizes work best because students have fun putting them on, and releases the tension by making everyone laugh. Set two tables, one with women's clothes, and another one with men's attire. Be sure there is enough space to walk in front of your desk, which could be used as the cash register area. From the very beginning identify yourself as the salesperson. You might want to dress accordingly for today's class, and select a student that happens to be dressed appropriately to be your assistant clerk. You and the student who is playing store clerk stand behind the cash register, and the customers walk to it. Help students trying on the clothes. Classroom doors can be designated as fitting rooms by posting signs reading *Señoras* and *Caballeros*.

New Commands

Use a different student for each clothing item.

Pruébate
- la chaqueta.
- los pantalones.
- el impermeable.
- la falda.

Ponte
- la camisa.
- la blusa.
- el suéter.
- el vestido.

Direct the following commands to the students that already have these items on.

Abróchate
- la blusa.
- la falda.
- la camisa.
- la chaqueta.

Desabróchate
- la blusa.
- la camisa.
- la chaqueta.

Súbete la cremallera
- del impermeable.
- **de la chaqueta.**
- de la falda.
- de los pantalones.

Bájate la cremallera
- de los pantalones.
- de la falda.

Quítate
- la chaqueta.
- el suéter.
- el impermeable.
- el vestido.

cliente

Select a salesperson and a customer from among the students.
- _____, levántate y toca al cliente.

dependiente (-a)
- _____, señala al depediente.
- _____, dibuja un círculo con el dedo alrededor del dependiente.
- _____, pon una cuchara sobre el cliente.
- _____, pon una cuchara sobre el dependiente.

More on the Present Indicative

—(A), empuja la mesa.

A pause.

—(B), empuja la mesa que empuja (A).
—(C), empuja la silla.

A pause.

—(D), empuja la silla que empuja (C).

Give the student a piece of paper with a long sentence written on it.

—(E), lentamente escribe esto en la pizarra.

A pause. While Student E is still writing, say:

—(F), borra lo que escribe (E).

Hold a book in your hand a say:

—Tengo un libro en la mano.

A pause.

—_____, señala el libro que tengo en la mano.

Introduction of
"¿Quién... ? / ¿A quién...? / ¿De quién... ?

Ask questions to the class. The expected answer is simply a student's name.

—(A), empuja (B) a la mesa.

A pause.

—¿A quién empujó (A) a la mesa?

—(C), dale la mano a (D).

A pause.

—¿A quién le dio la mano (C)?

Pointing to a student without calling him/her by name, say:

—Camina a la pizarra, y ponte de pie junto a la pizarra.

Then ask the class:

—¿Quién está junto a la pizarra?

—_____, siéntate en la mesa.

A pause.

—¿Quién está sentado en la mesa?

Look around the classroom and find a student with a certain piece of clothing. Then ask, for example:

—¿Quién lleva un suéter rojo?

Reading

Exhibit 2. Do orally first, before you distribute to students. Read and demonstrate each item on the sheet. Next class, pass out a copy of EXHIBIT 2 to each student. Be sure you cross out every item as you go, so you don't skip any. Have all the objects and pictures you need to do this ready, and in the right order, so you don't waste time looking for them.

Exhibit 2

VERBOS

come	ronca	abróchate	péinate
echa	depierta	desabróchate	cepíllate
bebe	mueve	súbete la cremallera	abraza
levanta	pellizca	bájate la cremallera	canta
pon	deja caer	quítate	baila
cuenta	mira	lávate	coge (to catch)
conduce	llora	sécate	bota
pita	sonríe	borra	ponte de pie
corre	pruébate	busca	lleva
duerme	ponte	sostén	enfádate

VOCABULARIO

la naranja	el tenedor	el peine	feliz / triste
la manzana	la taza	el estudiante	enfadado
la pera	el vaso	la mujer	mojado / seco
el agua	el triángulo	el hombre	derecha / izquierda
el café	el rectángulo	la foto	rápidamente / lentamente
la leche	los dientes	una vez (unas veces)	detrás de / delante de
el pan	la pasta de dientes	un dólar (unos dólares)	con
la cuchara	el cepillo de dientes	la cuerda	por la mitad
el cuchillo	el jabón	largo / corto	un poco de
	la toalla	alto / bajo	

NUMEROS

dieciséis (16)	treinta	noventa	seiscientos
diecisiete	cuarenta	cien (ciento)	setecientos
dieciocho	cincuenta	doscientos	ochocientos
diecinueve	sesenta	trescientos	novecientos
veinte	setenta	cuatrocientos	mil (1000)
veintiuno	ochenta	quinientos	un millón (1,000.000)

ESTRUCTURAS

1. Dale la mano a _____.
2. Levanta la mano izquierda.
3. Cierra los ojos.
4. Pon el vaso de agua delante de _____.
5. Da la vuelta a la derecha y pita.

Class Twelve

Props

books (yellow, red)
plastic chairs of different colors *(If you don't have them, substitute with clothes or books)*
spoon
video or slides of interior scenes in a clothing store
magazine with car ad
supermarket mailing
some text for a student to copy on the blackboard
department store plastic bags
picture of woman drying other woman's hair

picture of woman looking at paintings
picture of man laughing
picture of couple dancing
picture of woman driving the car
picture of woman brushing her teeth
picture of people singing
picture of man running
picture of woman jumping
picture of woman smiling

Setup

Display pictures on board for the second activity of this class. Set up classroom furniture and clothes for the clothing store activities. Put spoon on a chair.

Introduction of the Construction "¿Dónde está ...?"

The expected response is a short utterance.

—(A), **pon el libro amarillo debajo de la silla roja (negra, naranja ...).**

Pause.

—(B), **¿dónde está el libro amarillo?**
Answer: "**Debajo de la silla roja (negra, naranja ...)**"
—(C), **pon la silla amarilla (verde) junto a la silla negra (roja).**
—(D), **¿dónde está la silla amarilla?**
Answer: "**Junto a la silla negra (roja).**"
—(E), **pon el libro amarillo junto al libro rojo.**

Pause.

—(F), **¿dónde está el libro amarillo?**
Answer: "**Junto al libro rojo?**

Be sure the spoon is not on the table before you give the following command.

—(G), **pon la cuchara en la mesa.**

Pause.

—(H), **¿dónde está la cuchara?**
Answer: "**En la mesa.**"

More Practice with the Present Indicative

Notice how the relative clause structure is also embedded.

Hand the student some text to write on the board.
- —(A), **escribe esto en la pizarra.**
- —(B), **borra lo que (A) escribe.**
- —(A), **toca la mesa.**

Pause.
- —(B), **toca la mesa que (A) toca.**
- —(C), **lava la ventana.**

Pause.
- (D), **lava la ventana que lava (C).**

Using the pictures listed in the Props section, direct the students with commands to identify them.

- —Toca los hombres y las mujeres que cantan.
- —Señala el hombre que sonríe.
- —Señala la mujer que seca el pelo de la otra mujer.
- —Señala la mujer que mira los cuadros.
- —Dame la mujer que se ríe.
- —Señala al hombre y la mujer que bailan.
- —Pon a la mujer que conduce el coche en la mesa.
- —Pon a la mujer que se cepilla los dientes delante de las personas que cantan.
- —Camina al hombre que corre.
- —Tira la mujer que salta a (A).

The Clothing Store Experience

Take your students to a local department store. Introduce all the verbs and the clothing items in EXHIBIT 3 by giving commands to your students. Students normally enjoy this type of outing experience where the language can be experienced in real contexts.

A Video Presentation of a Clothing Store

Check out a portable video camera from your Media Center and go to a local department store. Request permission in advance from the management to do a few takes around the store. They don't normally have any objections if you identify yourself as a local teacher, and explain to them that the video will only be used in class for educational purposes.

Make sure you get a shot of all the clothing items and people listed in EXHIBIT 3. The class script that follows will give you an idea of the things you should have in mind while recording, and can also be used as text for narration. Later, back at school, do some video editing, and add sound by recording the text to go along with the images you have recorded. The other two alternatives for the sound track are, either to talk while you are recording at the store, or talk live in class when you play it back for the students.

To make sure students follow the narration, ask them questions about what they see. One possible way to do this is to pause every now and then, and get frames on the screen. Then, ask the question. You can also direct the student to point to certain people or items on the screen. It is always a good idea to let a student maninupale the controls, and thus you can also give commands about these too, such as **"Páralo"**, **"Sigue"**, etc. You can also do this live, with different students playing different roles (customer, salesperson). Here are some examples of the types of questions and/or commands you can use:

—¿**Cuál de las dos personas en la pantalla (junto a la mesa) es el dependiente?**

Pause.

—(A), **señala el cliente.**

—(B), **señala el dependiente.**

—(C), **por favor, dinos qué ropa lleva el cliente.**

—(D), **¿qué ves a la derecha de la pantalla (en la mesa)?**

And point to a certain item on the screen (on the table). Use the video to communicate the meaning of these verbs:

pagar

(A), **compra una camisa.** (PAUSE) **Ahora el cliente paga la camisa.**

(B), **camina a los grandes almacenes y compra unos pantalones.**

Ahora el cliente paga los pantalones. Cuando se paga la ropa, se le da dinero al dependiente.

El cliente le da dinero al dependiente.

El cliente paga la camisa.

comprar

El cliente compra una camisa.

El cliente compra unos pantalones.

vender

Los grandes almacenes venden ropa: pantalones, camisas, chaquetas ...

querer / gustar

_____, **mira esta chaqueta. ¿Quieres comprar esta chaqueta?**

_____, **mira estas botas. ¿Te gusta el color?**

Pause.

¿Quieres comprar estas botas?

Mira este bolso. Es muy grande (pequeño). ¿Quieres comprarlo?

robar

Have a small clothing item, a pair of socks or a scarf on hand, and quickly put it in your pocket. The say:

Algunas veces los clientes roban artículos en las tiendas.

Point to a customer on the screen (in the classroom) and ask:

¿Este cliente roba o compra los pantalones?

Si este hombre se mete los calcetines en el bolsillo sin pagar, eso se llama "robar".

Besides the clothing store, you can also do a few takes of other local businesses around town (supermarket, car dealership) to reinforce the meaning of some of these verbs. You can also use supermarket mailings, and magazine ads to illustrate the meaning. Here are some examples:

—**Este negocio vende coches.**

—**Cuando se va al supermercado se compra comida.**

—**Esta tienda vende comida.**

—**¿Qué comidas se compran en el supermercado?**

Using the video combine in a narrative form the verbs above (**pagar, comprar, vender, querer, gustar, mirar, robar**) with other clothing vocabulary such as:

- —manga—larga / corta.
- —talla—grande, mediana, pequeña
- —bolsillo
- —medias
- —gorra
- —sombrero
- —guantes

By watching the video students should be able to understand descriptive speech.

Practice With Personal Data

This exercise will involve listening, speaking, reading, and writing.

—Todos, escriban su nombre.
—Ahora escriban su apellido.

Give the following command to a male student.

—_____, escribe tu apellido en la pizarra.
Escribe "Sr." delante de tu apellido.

Pause.

—¿Cuál es tu apellido?

Give the following command to a female student.

—Escribe tu apellido en la pizarra.
—Escribe "Sra." delante de tu apellido.

Pause.

—¿Cuál es tu apellido?

Introduction of the Possessive Adjetives

Begin with 'mi' and 'tu.'

—Toca tu lápiz.
—Toca mi libro.
—Señala tu silla.
—Toca tu libro.
—Señala mi libro.

Add now "su."

—Mueve su papel.
—Mueve su silla..
—Señala su reloj.

Class Thirteen

Props

All items listed in Exhibit 3

Classroom Setup

Recreate again the environment of a clothing store by displaying clothes around the classroom. Have different students play customers, salespersons, cashiers, etc.)

Review of the Present Indicative

Begin with questions that require a short answer.
—(A), **levántate.**

Pause.
—(B), **¿está (A) de pie?**

Answer: "Sí," or "Sí, está de pie."
—(C), **¿llora (A)?**

Answer: "No," or "No, no llora."

Longer answers are required now.
—(A), **camina alrededor de la sala de clase; (B), escribe en la pizarra, y (C), canta.**

Pause. While the three students are performing these actions, ask other classmates:
—**¿Qué hace (A)?**
—**¿Qué hace (B)?**
—**¿Qué hace (C)?**

General Review

Recombine lexical items and grammatical features to produce new commands.

Review of the Clothing Store Experience

Direct students as follows:
—**Coge la camisa azul de manga larga.**

Pause.
—**¿De qué talla es?**

Pause.
—**¿Es tu talla?**

Pause.
—**¿Te está demasiado grande o demasiado pequeña?**

Pause.
—**Pruébate la gorra.**
—**Entra al probador.**

Point to one of the students involved in the action, and ask:
—¿Es esta mujer dependiente o cliente?
—Pregunta a la depediente cuánto cuesta la camisa.
—Caminemos al departamento de caballeros.

Pause. Pick a coat and put it next to Student A. Then Ask:
—¿Le sentaría bien una chaqueta de este color a (A)?

Pause.
—(B), ayúdale a (A) a ponerse la chaqueta.

And gesture for Student B to do this. After Student A has the coat on, ask the class:
—¿Está (A) guapo o feo con esa chaqueta?
—Señala las camisas.
—Señala los pantalones.
—Señala las corbatas.
—Señala las chaquetas.
—(A), ¿de qué talla son las camisas?
—(B) ayúdale a (A) a encontrar su talla en la sección de camisas.

Reading

Distribute **Exhibit 3** with all the clothing store vocabulary. The instructor reads each item twice and uses each in a familiar sentence. S/he can also write on the board representative sentences that students responded to in the clothing store video presentation.

Exhibit 3
LA ROPA. LOS GRANDES ALMACENES

VERBOS	**VOCABULARIO**	
probarse	el impermeable	el pijama
estar bien	la chaqueta	el botón (los botones)
llevar (ropa)	el suéter	la percha
mirar	la blusa	la manga (larga / corta)
comprar	la camisa	el bolsillo
vender	la camiseta	el pañuelo
pagar	la falda	el paraguas
	los pantalones (largos / cortos)	el abrigo
	la botas	el sombrero
	el vestido	la gorra
	la corbata	los guantes
	el cinturón	
	los calcetines	
	las medias	
	los zapatos	
	el bolso	el dinero ($$$)
		un cheque
		una tarjeta de crédito
		el cliente
		el dependiente

ESTRUCTURAS
mi / tu / su

demasiado grande / pequeño
largo(a) / corto(a)
talla (grande, mediana, pequeña)
color (marrón, gris, morado ...)
departamento de señoras
caballeros
probador

**PRESENT INDICATIVE
(SINGULAR FORMS)**

1. TOCAR (Yo) toc-o
   (Tú) toc-as
   (Usted / él / ella) toc-a
2. VENDER (Yo) vend-o
   (Tú) vend-es
   (Usted / él / ella) vend-e
3. ESCRIBIR (Yo) escrib-o
   (Tú) escrib-es
   (Usted / él / ella) escrib-e

1. —¿Te está bien la blusa?
   —No, me está pequeña.

2. —¿Qué ropa lleva el cliente?
   —Lleva una camisa de manga corta.

3. ¿Qué talla?
4. ¿Cuánto es?
5. ¿Cuántos dedos tienes?
6. ¿Dónde está el lápiz largo?
7. ¿Quién está en la pizarra?
8. ¿A quién le dió la mano _____?
9. ¿De quién es la camisa?
10. ¿Cómo se llama el estudiante alto?

Quiz 2 (Classes 6 - 13)

See **Tests** section at the end of the book.

Class Fourteen

Props

wall calendar (current year)

large flash-cards of different colors with days of the week

picture of a church

picture of a man drinking beer or a beer bottle (only for college classes)

large wall calendar with pictures of four seasons

Classroom Setup

Draw a big rectangle on the blackboard, and draw the current month as it appears on a wall calendar page. Use the whole board. Hang the calendar on the wall.

Asking Questions of Students

—(A), **toca la mesa.**

Pause.

—(A), ¿**qué haces?**
Answer: "Toco la mesa."
—(B), ¿**Qué hace (A)?**
Answer: "Toca la mesa."

Demonstrating the Present Indicative with Other Personal Pronouns such as: nosotros (-as), ustedes, ellos (as)

—(A) y (B), **caminen conmigo.**

Walk with them, and say:

—**Nosotros camin**amos.
—(C) y (D), **escriban en la pizarra.**

Pause.

—Ellos **escriben en la pizarra.**
—(E) y (F), **golpeen a (G).**

Pause. While Students E and F do this, look a them and say:

—Ustedes **golpean a (G).**

Introduction of the Days of the Week

Hang a big, current year montly calendar on the board, open to the current month, and display the large cards with the names of the days of the week written on them on the board as well. To avoid confusion, all time references will revolve around whichever day of the week you are teaching this class. The examples below are written assuming that today's class falls on a Monday, but you will need to change this if today is not Monday.

Point to the right day on the calendar, and say:

—**Hoy es lunes. Es el primer día de la semana.**
—(A), **coge el lunes y dáselo a (B).**

Pause.
        —(B), ¿qué día es hoy?

Point to Sunday, show a picture of people in church, and say:
        —El domingo es el último día de la semana.
        —Los domingos mucha gente va a la iglesia.
        —(C), rápidamente, coge el domingo y pónselo a (D) en la mano.

Pause.
        —(D), ¿qué día de la semana tienes en la mano?
        —¿Qué día fue ayer?

And point to Sunday.
        —¿Qué día es hoy?
        —Hoy es lunes. (E), muestra a la clase qué día es hoy.

Gesture to the student to show the Monday card.
        —Mañana es martes.

And point to Tuesday.
        —(F), corre a la pizarra, coge el martes y dáselo a (G).
        —(G), ¿qué día es mañana?
        —Hoy es lunes. Los lunes tenemos clase de español. ¿Tenemos clase de español los sábados?
        —¿Y los viernes?
        —_____, ¿estudias los sábados?

Point to Friday.
        —El viernes es el quinto día de la semana.

Show the picture of the man drinking beer, and say:
        —Los viernes, muchos estudiantes beben cerveza.
        —_____, ¿cuál es el primer día de la semana?
        —_____, ¿cuál es el segundo día de la semana?

Point to Wednesday.
        —El día después del martes es el miércoles.

Point to Thursday.
        —El día después del miércoles es el jueves.

Once the students have internalized the concept, and are responding well to the different days of the week, give them hypothetical situations. Hold up a particular card, and stand up in-between yesterday's and tomorrow's cards. Then say, for example:
        —Hoy es jueves.
        —Si hoy es jueves, ¿qué día es mañana?
        —Si hoy es jueves, ¿qué día fue ayer?

Finally, direct students to manipulate today, yesterday, and tomorrow. For instance:
        —(A), coge el lunes y tíraselo a (B).

The next set of questions refer to the different colors of the cards on which the names of days of the week are printed.

—¿De qué color es el lunes?
—¿Te gustan los lunes?
—¿De qué color es el martes?
—¿Te gustan los martes?

And so on with the rest of the week.

Introduction of the Months of the Year

Get the monthly calendar, and turn to the January page. Hold the calendar open, and say:
—Enero es el primer mes del año.

Turn the page, and continue with the rest of the months.
—Febrero es el segundo mes del año.
—Marzo es el tercer mes del año.
—Abril es el cuarto mes del año.
—Mayo es el quinto mes del año.

And so on.

Open the calendar to the current month, and pointing to today's date, say:
—Hoy estamos a _____ (day) de _____ (month) de _____ (year)
—Mañana es _____ (day of the week)

Tell students that in Spanish the day goes before the month. Using numbers (e.g. 12/7/91), write more dates on the board and have a student point to the right one as you read them. Also you can give dates and have the students find them in the calendar.

Crystal Ball Dates

Ask students to write down a date on a piece of paper, and through the wonders of parapsychology or magic, you guess the date they have written. You won't get it right, but they get to listen to dates and compare with what they have heard you say.

More with the Question Word "quién"

—(A), **toca a la persona que está sentada junto a ti.**

Pause. Ask the class:
—¿Quién está sentado (a) junto a (A)?
—(B), **ponte de pie delante de (C).**

Pause and ask the class:
—¿Quién está de pie delante de (C)?

Pause.

—(D), **pellizca a la persona que está sentada delante de (C).**
—(E), **toca la mesa.**

Pause.

—¿Quién toca la mesa?
—(F), **ponte de pie detrás de (G).**

Pause.

—¿Quién está detrás de (G)?

Class Fifteen

Props

flash-cards (days of the week)
calendar
newspaper
postcard
box of facial tissue
picture of your city or nearest big city
paper
scissors
picture of a famous person
your chair

FOR STORY ONE:
alarm clock
pajamas
picture of clothing store

Continued Practice Manipulating Days of the Week

Hang calendar and display flash cards as in yesterday's class.

—_____, cuenta los días de la semana.

—_____, ¿cuántos días tiene la semana?

—(A), dale el sábado a (B).

—_____, señala el lunes.

—_____, pon el miércoles junto al lunes.

Hold up the Saturday card, and ask:

—¿Es esta cartulina el lunes o el sábado, _____?

Hold up the Sunday card, and ask:

—¿Es esta cartulina el sábado o el domingo _____?

And put the card down.

—¿Qué día es hoy, _____?

Hold up the Friday card, and ask:

—¿Qué dice esta cartulina, _____?

More Practice with the Months of the Year

Hand the calendar to a student, and say:

—_____, abre el calendario en el mes de enero.

—(A), pasa el calendario a (B).

Pause.

—(B), abre el calendario en el mes de marzo.

—(C), muestra a los estudiantes el último mes del año.

—(D), muéstrame la fecha de tu cumpleaños.

Continue passing the calendar around the classroom until you have reviewed all the months.

New Commands

Act or gesture to communicate the meaning of the following verbs:

Lee
- el periódico.

And hand the student the newspaper.
- ¿De qué fecha es el periódico?
- ¿Es de hoy?
- Lee la postal.

And give him/her the postcard.

Write something on the board.
- Lee lo que escribí en la pizarra.

Abraza
- a (A).
- la mesa.
- Abrázate.

The verb "abrazar" has already been introduced. We put it here again for reinforcement.

Estornuda
- _____, estornuda. Toma un pañuelo.

Hand the student a tissue.
- _____, estornuda.
- Los demás digan: "Jesús María"
- _____, estornuda y vuelve la cabeza.

Mira por
- la ventana, _____.
- la puerta _____, y grita.

Review the Present Indicative with
yo / tú / usted / él / ella / nosotros (-as) / ustedes / ellos (-as)

Emphasize the verbal endings as you speak. While the action is being performed, elicit responses to your questions from the students, making sure they use the appropriate ending. The answers could be long or short, but they will have to use the right endings.

Show the picture of your city or neighboring major city, and say:
—Miren la foto de _____ (name of city).

Pause.
—Ustedes miran la foto de _____ (name of city).

Show the picture of a famous person.
—Ahora ustedes miran la foto de _____ (name of person).
—Todos miren por la ventana.

While everyone is doing this, ask:
>—¿Qué hacen?
>Answer: "Miramos por la ventana."
>—(A), lee los días de la semana.

Pause.
>—(B), ¿qué hace (A)?
>Answer: "Lee." or "Lee todos los días de la semana."
>—(C), abraza a (D).

Pause.
>—¿Qué haces (C)?
>Answer: "Abrazo a (D)."
>—(E), (F), y (G) bailen detrás de la mesa.

Pause. Ask the class:
>—¿Qué hacen ellos?
>Answer: "Bailan." or "Bailan detrás de la mesa."

Sit down and read the newspaper. While doing this, ask the students:
>—¿Qué hago yo?
>Answer: "Usted lee." or "Usted lee el periódico."

Hand the scissors to a student.
>—(A), córtale el pelo a (B).

Wait for the student to do this, and ask:
>—(A), ¿qué haces?
>Answer: "Le corto el pelo a (B)."
>—(B), ríete.

Pause.
>—(B), ¿qué haces?
>Answer: "Me río."

More on Possessive Adjectives

>—Toca tu silla.
>—Toca mi silla.

Point to a male student, and say:
>—_____, toca su silla.

Point to a female student, and say:
>—(A), toca su silla.

Pause.
>—(A), ¿qué haces?
>Answer: "Toco su silla."
>—(B), corta mi papel.

Pause.
>—(B), ¿qué haces?
>Answer: "Corto su papel."

Reading Stories

Do not distribute a copy of **Story 1** yet. First read twice to the students. The second time, provide some intonation and gestures to give the students some clues about the story. The students will listen. Before reading it a third time, ask for two volunteers (one boy, and one girl) to act it out, as you go over it once more. Do the narration aloud, but whisper their lines to the actors for them to say outloud to each other.

Set-up for **Story 1**:

1. Have the boy playing Mr. Smith pretend to get on some pajamas, and lay down on some chairs, as if they were a bed.
2. Mr. Smith is sleeping and the instructor begins the narration.
3. Just before you say "Es hora de levantarse," let the alarm go off.

As you proceed narrating the story, the students will continue acting out the text, and saying their lines as you prompt them.

After the dramatization, ask individual students questions about the story that call for a yes/no answer. E.g. "¿Mira el Sr. Smith por la ventana?" Next ask questions that require a longer response, such as "¿Qué hace el Sr. Smith?" You can use the rest of the questions printed after the story.

Finally, distribute copies of the story, and let them examine it silently. Have the students read together the story aloud, and read each question twice. The instructor writes the answer to each question on the board, and students copy them on their notebooks.

STORY 1

El Sr. Smith duerme. Es la hora de levantarse. Se quita el pijama y se pone la ropa. Mira por la ventana y ve que está lloviendo. Dice a la Sra. Smith:

—¿Dónde está el paraguas?

la Sra. Smith dice:

—¡Mira debajo de la mesa!

El Sr. Smith dice:

—No está aquí.

La Sra. Smith dice:

—¡Mira en la silla!

Ahora el Sr. Smith está enfadado. Grita, salta tres veces, y corre a la puerta.

PREGUNTAS

1. ¿Está el Sr. Smith en unos grandes almacenes?
2. ¿Compra ropa la Sra. Smith?
3. ¿Está lloviendo?
4. ¿Qué busca el Sr. Smith?
5. ¿Dónde dice la Sra. Smith que busque el paraguas?
6. ¿Está el Sr. Smith feliz, triste o enfadado?
7. ¿Por qué está el Sr. Smith enfadado?
8. ¿Qué hace para mostrar su enfado?

Class Sixteen

Props

2 paper towels
pictures of a handsome man, ugly man, pretty woman, ugly woman
picture of a man or a woman thinking
big box
small box (one of the boxes empty, the other one full)
long piece of string
short piece of string
drawings or pictures of faces (sad, happy, scared, nervous, angry, tired)
picture of a snake
picture of Frankestein or some other monster

2 glasses
big paper bag
small paper bag
big book
small book
water
dirty white paper
clean white paper
colored paper (pink, light blue, dark blue)
scissors
$5 or $10 bill (put it on the table)
purse
basket ball
bottle (to fill glasses)

Review of the Present Indicative

Quickly elicit a chain of short and long responses from two individual students.
- ¿Quién está sentado (-a) a tu derecha?

Tell a student to drink. Then ask:
- ¿Qué haces?
- ¿Estudias español?
- (B), ponte de pie en una silla.

Pause.
- ¿Está (B) de pie en una silla?
- Escribe tu nombre en el papel de la mesa.

While s/he does it, ask the next two questions.
- ¿Qué escribes?
- ¿Dónde escribes tu nombre?
- Siéntate.

Pause.
- ¿Junto a quién estás sentado (-a)?

Show picture of woman or man thinking. "Think" is now introduced for the first time.
- Este hombre piensa.

Show the picture of a man thinking, such as Rodin's Thinker. But if you are unable to find a suitable picture, simply get on a thinking posture yourself, putting your right hand on your chin to communicate the meaning of the following question.
- ¿Piensas?
- ¿En qué piensas?

If the student does not understand, you could draw a picture of a face on the board with a bubble coming out of the head, and a big question mark inside.
- (B) y (C), pónganse de pie en sus sillas.

Pause.
- ¿Dónde están de pie (B) y (C)?

"Escucha" is a new word, so act out the meaning of the following verb by putting your hand next to your ear.
- (B), ¿escuchas?
- ¿Duerme (C)?
- (A), ponte de pie.

Pause.
- ¿Dónde está de pie (A)?
- (D) y (E), lean sus libros.

Pause.
- ¿Qué hacen ellos?
- ¿Saltas?
- ¿Escribe (D) mi nombre?

Review Contrasts Through Commands

—Todos, levántense.

Pause.

—(A), ponte de pie entre una persona alta y una persona baja.

Wet a piece of towel paper.

—(B), dale la toalla mojada a (C), y dame a mí la toalla seca.

Review Contrasts Through Short Answers

Hold up one of the two pieces of string, and ask:
—¿Es la cuerda larga o corta?

Hold up one of the two pieces of towel paper, and ask:
—¿Está la toalla mojada o seca?

Then into "yes" or "no" Answers

Pretend to spill some water on the floor.
—¿Está el suelo mojoado?

Answer: "Sí."
—¿Está la mesa mojada?

Answer: "No."

New Contrasts

guapo / feo
- Pon la foto del hombre guapo en la pizarra, y la foto del hombre feo en la cabeza de _____.
- Pon la foto de la mujer guapa en la ventana, y la foto de la mujer fea en la mesa.

grande / pequeño

Put the two boxes on the floor.
- Pon a (A) junto a la caja grande, y a (B) junto a la caja pequeña.
- Dale el libro pequeño a (B), y el libro grande a (C).
- Abre la bolsa grande, y cierra la bolsa pequeña.

lleno / vacío

Pretend to fill up of the glasses with water, then say:
—Pon el vaso lleno de agua en el vaso vacío.
—Pon el vaso lleno de agua en la cabeza de _____.
—Lleva el vaso vacío a la ventana.

claro / oscuro

Show the two pieces of blue paper.
- Coge el papel azul oscuro y córtalo en tres pedazos.
- Señala a alguien que lleva un suéter azul oscuro.
- ¿Quién lleva pantalones oscuros?

limpio / sucio

Show a white, dirty piece of paper, and then say:
- Este papel está sucio.

Show clean piece of paper.
- Este papel está limpio.

Rub your finger on a window glass, show the finger to the students, and ask:
- ¿Está la ventana limpia o sucia?

Point to the floor.
- ¿Está el suelo limpio o sucio?

Also show pictures of clean or dirty shoes, floors, bikes, etc. if you can find them, and ask questions like,
- ¿Está el zapato limpio o sucio?
- ¿Está la bicicleta limpia o sucia?

Emotional or Affective States of Being

The instructor demonstrates an emotional response by acting it out, and shows a picture. Then asks the students to act it out.

enfado
- Estoy enfadado.

And act as if you were angry. Then show the picture of the angry man.
- Este hombre está enfadado.

Pause.
- _____, dale la vuelta a la foto del hombre enfadado.
- (A), golpea a (B) en el brazo.

Pause.
- (B), enfádate.

tristeza

Show the picture of the sad woman.
- La mujer de esta foto está triste. Ella está así. Mírenme a la cara. Estoy triste.

And get sad.
- Estoy triste.

Look for a student who has a purse. Let's identify him or her as Student B.
- (A), coge el bolso de (B), y llévatelo a tu silla.

Pause.
- (B), ponte triste.
- Ahora llora.

felicidad
- _____, corre a la mesa, coge diez dólares y dámelos.

Pause.
- Ahora estoy feliz.

And get happy.
- _____, busca una foto de una cara feliz, y ponla junto a la cara triste.
- Dibuja una cara feliz en la pizarra.

Direct the following command to a female student.
- (A), dile a (B) que él es guapo.
- (B), cuando ella te diga que tú eres guapo, pon una cara feliz.

nerviosismo

Show picture of a nervous person or give a student a piece of paper and a pen, and say:
- Este estudiante va a examinarse en la escuela. Está nervioso (-a).

Pause.
- Cuando yo estoy nervioso golpeo el suelo con el pie.

And tap your foot.

(A), muéstranos lo que haces cuando estás nervioso.

Pause.
- ¿Golpeas el suelo con el pie?
- ¿Te comes las uñas?

And bite your nails.
- ¿Te rascas la cabeza?

And scratch your head.
- ¿Te rizas el pelo con el dedo?
- ¿Te paseas rápidamente de un lado a otro?

And pace back and forth across the room.
- (B), ¿qué haces cuando estás nervioso? A ver...

cansancio

Show a picture of someone who looks tired, say a picture of marathon runner after completing a race, or a woman working on the fields.

- Este hombre ha corrido muchos kilómetros. Está cansado.
- Esta mujer ha estado trabajando todo el día. Está cansada.
- Después de trabajar todo el día, estoy cansado.

Act tired.

- (A), salta diez veces rápidamente.

Pause.

- (A), ¿estás cansado?
- (B), ¿crees que (A) está cansado?

susto

Get the picture of the snake, walk to a student and show it to her. Then say:

- Esta chica acaba de ver la serpiente. Está asustada.

Do the same with the monster's picture.

- Esta chica acaba de ver a Frankestein. Está asustada.

Walk to a student, stand very close, raise your fist, and scream:

- Voy a golpearte. ¡Asústate! ¡Grita!

Hand the student the big book and say:

- (A), golpéame con el libro.

Pause.

- Mírenme a la cara.

Look scared.

- (A) me asusta. Estoy asustado.

Play Statue

After you have introduced all the emotional states, you can play this game by asking the whole class to walk around the classroom. When you state a command such as "enfádate," everyone stops walking, and freezes posing as a statue with the appropriate expression on their face and body. This dramatic exercise can be also played with students at their seats, without walking.

A variation could be to draw faces showing emotional states on their notebooks, as you call the commands.

General Review

Review rapidly everything from the beginning. Include verbs, parts of the body, colors, numbers, clothing, opposites, prepositions, possessives, present continuous. Here is a sample.

—Ponte la cuerda larga alrededor del cuello.

Pretend to fill one of the glasses with water, and fill one of the boxes with paper.

—Pon el vaso lleno de agua en la caja vacía.

—Señala un estudiante que lleve un suéter claro.

—Señala un estudiante que lleve unos pantalones oscuros.

—Dibuja una cara feliz en la pizarra.

While the student is doing this, ask the following questions, and wait for a response to each one.
>—¿Qué haces?
>—¿Qué dibujas?
>—¿Dónde dibujas la cara?

Ask the students to draw a sad face on their notebooks.
>—Dibuja una cara triste.

Quickly say the next four commands that referred to the task of drawing the sad face on the notebook. You provide feedback by drawing on the board.
>—Dibújale las orejas.
>—Dibújale la nariz.
>—Dibújale el pelo.
>—Dibújale los dientes.
>—Cuenta las caras felices de los estudiantes de este curso.
>—Escribe el número 86 en el papel rosa y dáselo a _____.
>—¿Quién está sentado junto a _____?
>—(A), Siéntate en el balón de baloncesto.
>—¿Dónde está sentado (A)?
>—Señala a una estudiante de pelo largo.
>—Quítate los zapatos.

Class Seventeen

Props

pencils (one short, one long)
sweaters (one light, one dark; you can borrow from students)
pictures or drawings of girls (one beautiful, one ugly)
big box
bottle
dance music
tape player
$1 bill
cassette with recordings in several languages
book
paper cup
paper plate

New Commands

Baila
- conmigo.
- con (A) y (B).
- alrededor de la mesa.

Toca

Students can mime playing the musical instruments.
- la guitarra.
- **el piano.**
- el violín.
- la trompeta.
- el trombón.
- el tambor.
- el saxofón.
- el clarinete.
- el acordeón.
- la armónica.

Canta
- una canción de los Beatles.

If the student is having difficulty remembering a tune, you can always lead with "Old McDonald Had a Farm."
- y baila alrededor de la mesa.

Play the dance music.

Actúa
- como si estuvieras loco.
- como si estuvieras borracho.

Stumble across the room yourself.
- como si estuvieras feliz.
- como si estuvieras triste.
- como si estuvieras nervioso.
- como si estuvieras cansado.

- como si estuvieras asustado.

Habla
- inglés.
- español.
- francés.
- alemán.
- chino.
- ruso.
- portugués.
- japonés.
- italiano.

You can also play a tape with segments recorded in different languages, or read a piece yourself if you have a reading knowledge of some of the languages above.

Rompe
- la botella.
- el lápiz.
- el vaso.
- la silla.
- la mesa.
- le la cabeza.
- el plato.

Review of Opposites and State of Being Words

Direct a tall student (A) to stand in the middle of the classroom, and ask a short student (B) to stand next to him, i.e.,

—(A), ponte de pie en medio de la sala.

—(B), corre al hombre alto que está de pie en el medio de la sala, y tócale el brazo.

Pause.

alto / bajo

—(C), tócale la nariz al hombre bajo que está de pie junto al hombre alto.

largo / corto

—Tírale el lápiz corto a (A) y el lápiz largo a (B).

claro / oscuro

—Dale el suéter oscuro a (C) y el suéter claro a (D).

Use the appropriate pictures for the next command.

guapa / fea

—Pon la chica guapa en la silla de (E), y la chica fea en el libro de (F).

feliz / triste

—_____, ponte feliz, canta y ríete.

—(A), golpea a (B) en la pierna.

Pause.

—(B), enfádate y llora.

—(C), dale a (B) un dólar y ponte triste. Llora.

Introduction of poder

Set the big box in the middle of the classroom, and say:
—Yo puedo saltar sobre la caja.

Do it.
—(A), ¿puedes saltar sobre esta caja?

Answer: "Sí."
—Entonces... salta.

After (A) has jumped over it, ask:
—(B), ¿puede (A) saltar sobre la caja?
—(C), dile a (A) que salte sobre la caja.

Put a chair next to the box.
—(A), ¿puedes saltar sobre la caja y la silla?

Let the student try his luck. The atmosphere of this exercise should be that of a three-ring circus when an artist is doing an "even harder yet" routine. You, of course, play the role of the ring leader.

To the following questions students are to answer "yes" or "no".
—¿Puedes tocar la mesa?
—¿Puedes tocar el techo?
—Ponte de pie en la silla.

Pause.
—¿Puedes tocar el techo ahora?
—¿Puedes ponerte de pie en la silla?
—¿Puedes ponerte de pie en el suelo?
—¿Puedes ponerte de pie en el techo?
—¿Puedes caminar a la ventana?
—¿Puedes caminar a la pared?
—¿Puedes caminar en el techo?
—¿Puedes caminar sobre el agua?

Introduction of saber

—¿Sabes tocar la guitarra?

If the student says yes, then say:
—Pues bien... toca la guitarra.

The student should strum an imaginary guitar.
—¿Sabes tocar el piano?

Pause.
—Bien... toca el piano.
—¿Sabes dibujar un gato?

Pause.
—Pues bien... dibuja un gato.

Have the student draw a cat on the board.

Role Reversal

Now give students a chance to ask you or other students *poder / saber* questions. Give them first a few examples:

—¿Puede sentarse en la silla?

Answer: "Sí."

—¿Puede sentarse en el techo?

Answer: "No."

—(A), ¿puedes caminar en el suelo?

Answer: "Sí."

—(B), ¿puedes caminar en el techo?

Answer: "No."

Class Eighteen

Props

4 or 5 flowers
chalk
textbook of different subjects
picture of child with birthday cake

Review

Select one student at a time and fire five to ten commands and questions such as:

—(A), tócate la nariz.

Pause.

—¿Qué haces?
—(B), empuja la silla.

Pause

—¿Qué hace (B)?
—¿Está el suelo mojado o seco?
—¿Está la ventana limpia?
—Coge la tiza y rómpela.
—¿Cuál es tu apellido?
—(C), camima a la pizarra y escribe tu nombre.
—Dibuja una flor debajo de tu nombre.
—¿Dónde está la flor?
—¿Puedes tocar el techo?
—¿Eres estudiante?
—¿Qué estudias?

Help the student answer that question by showing her the books she has under her desk, or by showing her, one at a time, the textbooks you have brought to class today as props. As you show one, ask,

—¿Estudias matemáticas?
—¿Estudias historia?

And so on.

To communicate the meaning of next command, show picture of child with birthday cake, as you ask:

—¿Cuántos años tiene?

Follow up with

—¿Cuántos años tienes?
—Coge las flores y cuéntalas.
—¿Cuántas flores tienes?
—Mueve la cabeza.

Role reversal

Ask two students to ask you one question and give you a command or two.

Pancho Carrancho

Play this game created by Ramiro García (See García's book, Instructor's Notebook: How to Apply TPR for Best Results, 2nd. ed., Los Gatos, CA: Sky Oaks Productions, 1988). You begin by making a statement about Pancho Carrancho, such as "Pancho Carrancho compra una chaqueta." A student will then deny your statement, and come up with one of his own: "No, Pancho Carrancho, no compra una chaqueta; Pancho Carrancho come." The next student may say: "No, Pancho Carrancho no come; él golpea al dependiente en la cabeza." Go around the classroom until every student has had a turn. Also, another way of playing the game and making it more exciting by keeping everybody on their toes, is asking each student to select a term from a given lexical field that has already being introduced, such as parts of the body, the clothing store, etc. and writing these words on the board. You begin by selecting a word from the board at random, and making a statement using that word. The student who picked that word will have to respond within two seconds, by putting your statement in the negative, and providing another one using another word from the board. If a student takes more than two seconds to respond, that student is eliminated, and you cross out his/her word from the board. The winner, of course, is the person whose word remains on the board last.

Later on you can play this game with fruits and vegetables, professions, etc. You should begin the game providing a sintactic structure like a statement in the present tense, as in the examples above, or commands, or past tense, that the students are familiar with. This game gives them a chance to practice that structure as well as reviewing a whole lexical field.

You can use this game periodically throughout the term. Students can thus appreciate their progress by seeing how their listening and speaking skills get better every time you play the game. Needless to say, you should not expect perfect pronunciation at this stage of training.

Class Nineteen

Props

English book
grammar book
calendar
purse

Setup

Using class time as a reference, e.g. 9:00 a.m., draw clocks on the board showing different times like 8:45 a.m., 9;00 a.m., and 9:15 a.m. to visualize meaning for *temprano, a tiempo,* and *tarde*.

Reading Stories

Before you begin class, make sure the classroom door, windows, lights, chalkboard, etc. are as described in **Story2**. Thus, you can point to these items when reading the story, and make its meaning more plain. Fill the blanks with students' names, and read the story aloud twice. As you read the story a third time, the students mentioned will act it out.

Next ask the questions about the story printed at the end. For variety, ask the students to write their answers in their notebooks to some of the questions.

At this point, distribute a copy of the story to each student to be read silently. In addition to reading the story, the students will also read each question that was asked about the story. For question #2, point to the clock to show the meaning of this question, and use class time as a reference point.

STORY TWO

Los estudiantes están en clase. Han llegado temprano y esperan al (a la) profesor (-a) _____. El / Ella normalmente llega a tiempo. La sala de clase es grande. Las luces están encendidas y la puerta está abierta. El aire acondicionado / la calefacción está encendido (-a). Las ventanas están cerradas. La pizarra está sucia y (A) la borra. (B) está sentada en la mesa. Lee su libro de español. (C) está sentada junto a (B) y estudia una lección de gramática. (D) y (E) hablan y se ríen. (F) está cansado y no hace nada.

QUESTIONS

1. ¿Dónde están los estudiantes?
2. ¿Llega normalmente el / la profesor (-a) a tiempo o tarde?
3. ¿Borra alguien la pizarra?
4. ¿Es la clase grande o pequeña?
5. ¿Cómo están las luces?
6. ¿Está la pizarra limpia o sucia?
7. ¿Quién está sentada en la mesa?
8. ¿Qué lee?
9. ¿Quién está sentada junto a (B)?
10. ¿Quién estudia una lección de gramática?
11. ¿Qué hacen (D) y (E)?
12. ¿Cómo está (F)? ¿Qué hace?

Review

If students are not wearing the clothing items included in this review session, take a good look at the clothes they are wearing today before you begin this exercise. Then change the commands or questions to suit their outfits.

lleva
- Señala al estudiante que lleva una chaqueta marrón.
- Mira al estudiante que lleva la camisa verde clara.
- Abraza al estudiante que lleva el suéter rojo.
- Dale la mano a la persona que lleva una camisa de manga larga.
- ¿Quién lleva una falda?
- ¿Qué ropa lleva (A)?
- ¿Qué ropa lleva (B)?

Review with Questions Words—qué, quién, dónde

Hand a student a book, and ask:

—¿Qué sostiene él?

—¿Qué mira ella?

—¿Quién está sentado junto a _____?

—¿Dónde está tu bolso?

Review of the Days of the Week

—¿Qué día es hoy?

—Hoy es (**day of the week**).

—_____, ¿estás feliz los (**day of the week**) (-s)?

—¿Estás feliz los viernes?

—Mañana es (**day of the week**).

—_____, ¿vas a venir a clase mañana?

Reading

Distribute **Exhibit 4** to each student. Read each item twice and then use it in a sentence.

Exhibit 4

DIAS DE LA SEMANA	MESES DEL AÑO	VERBOS	
el lunes	enero	hace	piensa
el martes	febrero	está	escucha
el miércoles	marzo	tiene	llega
el jueves	abril	dice	toca (un instrumento
el viernes	mayo	lee	musical)
el sábado	junio	saca	habla
el domingo	julio	estudia	actúa
	agosto		rompe
	septiembre		
	octubre		
	noviembre		
	diciembre		

VOCABULARIO

la persona	el violín	la iglesia	cansado
el coche	español	primer (primero)	borracho
el supermercado	inglés	segundo	asustado
la comida	francés	tercero (tercer)	guapo / feo
el periódico	alemán	cuarto	lleno / vacío
la postal	chino	último	limpio / sucio
el piano	la caja	loco	claro / oscuro
la guitarra	la cerveza	nervioso	temprano / a tiempo / tarde
			grande / pequeño

ESTRUCTURAS

1. ¿Qué día es hoy?
   Hoy es martes.
2. Mañana es miércoles.
   Ayer fue lunes.
3. ¿Cuál es la fecha?
   19 de octubre.
4. ¿Cuántos años tienes?
   15 años.
5. ¿Puedes tocar el techo?
   Sí (no).
6. ¿Sabes tocar el piano?
   Sí (no).

PRESENT INDICATIVE (PLURAL FORMS)

toc-ar
(nosotros / -as) toc-**amos**
(ustedes / ellos / -as) toc-**an**

vend-er
(nosotros / -as) vend-**emos**
(ustedes / ellos / -as) vend-**en**

escrib-ir
(nosotros / -as) escrib-**imos**
(ustedes / ellos / -as) escrib-**en**

Midterm Exam (Classes 1 - 19)

See the **Tests** section at the end of the book.

Class Twenty

Props

pencil

occupation cards (cut pictures from magazines, and paste them on a piece of cardboard):
mechanic • doctor • nurse • lawyer • engineer

Review

Using commands, move individual students rapidly with utterances containing each verb previously used in any class session.

New material (the past tense)

As with other grammar features, the past tense is also imbedded in the imperative. Pause for students to perform the command before reporting the action in the past tense.

—(A), tira tu lápiz al suelo.

Pause.

—(B), coge el lápiz que (A) tiró al suelo.
—(C), escribe el número 6 en la pizarra.

Pause.

—Señala con el dedo el número que escribiste.
—(D), señala el número que escribió (C).
—(E), cierra la ventana.

Pause.

—(F), abre la ventana que (E) cerró.
—(G), escribre el número 83, y (H), escribe el número 64.

Pause.

—(I), borra el número que escribió (G).

New material (occupational vocabulary items)

Display the three magazine pictures of occupations that you prepared for class today.

mecánico
- (A), muestra el mecánico a (B).

Pause.

- (B), quítale el mecánico a (A) y ponlo en la cabeza de (C).

médico
- (D), tírale el médico a (E).

Pause.

- (E), pon el médico debajo de tu silla.

enfermera
- Todos miren a la enfermera. _____, corre al frente de la clase, coge la enfermera y tírala a la ventana.

Introduce "abogado" and "ingeniero" by giving commands to students to manipulate the occupation cards.

Class Twenty-One

Props

paper
picture for Exhibit 5:
Driver's License or Social Security Number card
picture of couple getting married
picture of child and birthday cake
calendar
occupation cards for all items listed in Exhibit 6

More with the Preterite Tense

—(A), siéntate en la silla.

Pause.

—(B), ve al estudiante que se sentó en la silla.
—(C), tira el papel al suelo.

Pause.

—(D), coge el papel que él/ella tiró al suelo.
—(E), levántate.

Pause. Then say to the class:

—El/ella se levantó.

Pause.

—(F) y (G), levántense.

Pause.

—Ellos se levantaron.
—(H), levántate, ve a la pizarra, escribe tu nombre y siéntate en tu silla.

Pause.

—(H) se levantó, fue a la pizarra, escribió su nombre, y se sentó en su silla.

Continue the exercise with ten verbs varied as to person (i.e. yo, tú, Ud., él, ella, nosotros, (-as), Uds., ellos (-as) emphasizing the change in the verb associated with past actions:

—(A), pon la foto en el suelo y salta sobre ella.

Pause.

—(B), coge la foto sobre la que saltó (A).
—(C), (D) y (E), levántense.

Pause.

—Se levantaron.
—¡Siéntense todos!

Pause.

―Ustedes se sentaron.
―(F), camina a la ventana.

Pause.

―(F), ¿qué hiciste?

Help the student with the answer:

―"Caminé a la ventana."

Pause.

―(G), ¿qué hizo (F)?

Answer: "Caminó a la ventana."

More on Occupations

Again direct students manipulating occupation cards, e.g.:

―Pon al profesor junto al ingeniero.

Continue with the rest of the cards until you introduce all occupations in **Exhibit 6** that you will find in Class 22.

Reading and Writing

Read each command or question from **Exhibit 5** and elicit a response before you distribute the exhibit. Then students silently read each item on the sheet and write a response.

Exhibit 5

1. Escribe tu apellido.
2. Escribe la fecha.
3. Dibuja un círculo.
4. Escribe tu dirección.
5. Escribe tu número de teléfono.
6. Escribe el número siete arriba, a la derecha de este papel.
7. Escribe tu edad y dibuja una línea debajo. ¿Cuántos años tienes?
8. ¿Eres estudiante?
9. ¿Qué estudias?
11. ¿Está el suelo sucio?
12. ¿Está la puerta abierta?
13. ¿Qué ropa llevas?
14. ¿Estás casado (-a), soltero (-a), o divorciado (-a)?
15. Dobla este papel por la mitad.

Class Twenty-Two

Props

Occupation cards for all items listed in Exhibit 6

Review of Occupations

Hand each student an occupation card selected at random. Keep one card for yourself, show the card to the class, and mime the profession as a hint that they will be next. Give the students a few minutes to think about how best to act out the occupation in their cards. Once they are ready, have each person mime the type of work of the occupation represented in his/her card. If a certain profession could be better pantomimed by having two people, encourage the students to use a classmate for that purpose. You, the instructor, will then try to guess, in Spanish, the occupation being performed. If after a while, a student fails to communicate the meaning of his/her profession, she or he can show the card as a last resort, and you or the class will then name the profession in Spanish.

Reading

Distribute **Exhibit 6** to each student. Give an occupation card to each student, and ask them to keep it visible to the rest of the class. Then ask

—¿Es (A) médico?

If Student A is indeed holding the doctor card, the answer will be "Sí."

—¿Es (B) bombero?

Answer: "Sí or No," depending on whether or not he is holding the firefighter card.

Another way to review professions is to line up all occupation cards standing on the floor, against the wall, and ask each student to pick up one.

Exhibit 6
PROFESIONES

VOCABULARIO

1. estudiante
2. profesor (maestro)
3. médico
4. enfermera
5. dentista
6. mecánico
7. ama de casa
8. camarero (mesero)
9. cajero
10. dependiente
11. abogado
12. policía
13. bombero
14. secretaria
15. agricultor
16. camionero
17. barbero (peluquero)
18. (el) cura
19. monja
20. soldado
21. farmacéutico
22. piloto
23. periodista
24. pintor
25. escultor
26. panadero
27. carnicero
28. cocinero
29. minero
30. ingeniero
31. arquitecto
32. músico
33. cantante
34. cartero
35. presidente
36. bibliotecario
37. zapatero

ESTRUCTURAS

1. —¿En qué trabajas?
   —Soy cocinero.

2. —¿Es John dentista?
   —Sí (no).

Class Twenty-Three

Props

overhead transparency of Exhibit 7
clean cloth to wash windows
I.D. card (for Exhibit 7)

Classroom Setup

door open   chair next to board
window open   chair next to wall

Review of the Preterite Tense

Without announcing anything, but making sure you have the attention of the student, perform the following actions cleanly and distinctively:

  levantarse   ir a la pizarra
  escribir la fecha   sentarse

Then report on what you did to the class, i.e.
    —Me levanté; fui a la pizarra; escribí la fecha, y me senté."

Now address the students with the following commands. As usual when practicing the past tense, pause until the actions have been completed to ask the questions.

    —(A), ve a la ventana, lávala, y después, apaga la luz, y siéntate.

Pause.

    —¿Qué hizo (A)?

Answer: "Fue a la ventana, la lavó, después apagó la luz y se sentó."

    —(A), ¿qué hiciste?

Answer: "Fui a la ventana, la lavé, después apagué la luz y me senté."

Introduction of Negation Combined with the Preterite Tense

Make sure one of the doors of your classroom is open.

    —(A), camina a la puerta pero no la cierres.

Pause.

    —(B), cierra la puerta que (A) no cerró.

If the windows in your classroom open, make sure one of the windows is open. Otherwise, ask a student to pretend opening a window before giving the following command.

    —(C), camina a esa ventana pero no la cierres.

Pause.

    —(D), cierra la ventana que (C) no cerró.
    —(E), toca la silla que está junto a la pizarra, pero no toques la silla que está junto a la pared.

Pause.

    —(F), toca la silla que (E) no tocó.

Reading and Writing Personal Information

Distribute a copy of **Exhibit 7** to each student and put your transparency on the overhead projector. First read each item aloud and fill in your personal information on the overhead to illustrate the procedure. Begin with last name, write on the overhead, and then ask a student:

—(A), ¿cuál es tu apellido?

Pause for the student to answer. Then point to the right blank in the transparency and say:

—Bien, escribe aquí en la tarjeta tu apellido.

Next, have the students systematically fill in the rest of their personal data on the sheet.

Antoher way to do this exhibit is to stage it. A student has been taken to a police station for questioning, and you, the police officer, is asking the student all the questions in the exhibit, and writing the answers down on a form.

Exhibit 7

1. Nombre _____
2. Dirección _____
3. Loculated _____
4. Provincia (Estado) _____
5. Districto Postal _____
6. Teléfono (____) _____
7. Número de la Seguridad Social _____
8. Edad _____
9. Sexo: ____ Varón ____ Hembra
10. Estado Civil: ___ Soltero ___ Casado ____ Divorciado ____ Viudo
11. Lugar de nacimiento _____
12. Fecha de nacimiento _____ Día / Mes / Año
13. Profesión _____

Class Twenty-Four

Props

newspaper

two clocks (one digital)

flask cards with clocks at the quarter hour drawn on them (1:15, 8:45, 3:45, 5:45, 6:15 and 6:45)

pencil

red paper (for Exhibit 8)

transparency of class schedule (for Exhibit 9, question "What are you studying?")

textbooks of different subjects

picture of boy and birthdate cake (for Exhibit 9, question "How old are you?")

picture of people married (Exhibit 9)

picture of breakfast (a color picture of eggs, coffee, pastries, fruit, etc. for Exhibit 9)

Review of Occupations

Play "Pancho Carrancho" with occupations. Each student gives a you a profession and you write it on the board. The structure will be "Pancho Carrancho es carpintero." "No, Pancho Carrancho no es carpintero, es dentista," and so on.

Continue with the Preterite Tense Requiring Short Answer Responses (sí/no)

—(A), **toca la silla.**

Pause.

—**¿rompió (A) la silla?**

Answer: "No."

—(B), **corre a la puerta.**

Pause.

—**¿Se rompió la pierna (B)?**

Answer: "No."

—(C), **lee el periódico.**

Pause.

—**¿Leyó (C) el periódico?**

Answer: "Sí."

—(D) **y** (E), **empujen a** (F).

Pause.

—**¿Empujaron** (D) **y** (E) **a** (F)?

Answer: "Sí."

Reading

Do **Exhibit 8** orally first as commands. Then distribute Exhibit 8. Read each item aloud twice. An individual student will read a command from the left column of the exhibit, which another will act out. Then the student who has read the command will tell what has been done by reading the corresponding item on the right column.

Exhibit 8

Robert, camina a la mesa.	Robert caminó a la mesa.
, grita.	gritó.
, levanta la mano.	levantó la mano.
, tírame el lápiz.	me tiró el lápiz.
, coge el papel rojo de la mesa.	cogió el papel rojo de la mesa.
, golpea a _____ en el brazo.	golpeó a _____ en el brazo.
, dibuja una cara feliz.	dibujó una cara feliz.

Telling Time

Display the two clocks in full view of the class, and call on a student to use one of the clocks, and you use the other. If the class is small, do this exercise with students sitting around a table. You say the time and set the hands for the correct time. The student will do the same. After the student is beginning to get the idea, let the student do it first, and then you set your clock to the correct time for immediate feedback.

—Pon el reloj a las seis.
—Pon el reloj a las seis y media.
—Ahora son las nueve en punto.
—Pon el reloj a las siete y media.

Pause.

—_____, ¿qué hora es?

Answer: "Son las siete y media."

—Pon el reloj a las doce en punto.

Pause.

—_____, ¿qué hora es?

Answer: "Son las doce en punto."

Continue with Time

Have students draw clocks or write down different times with numbers at the hour or half hour, then ask them or have a student ask them,

—¿Qué hora es?

For example:

—Pon el reloj a la una y cuarto.
—Pon el reloj a las nueve menos cuarto.
—Pon el reloj a las cuatro menos cuarto.
—Pon el reloj a las seis y cuarto.
—Pon el reloj a las siete menos cuarto.

Introduction of Fine Detail in Telling Time

Display flash cards, each with a drawing of a clock at the quarter hour, and the time written on them in a digital fashion at the bottom.

—(A), **dale la una y cuarto a (B).**

—_____, **coge las nueve menos cuarto y ponlas debajo de la silla.**

—_____, **pon las cuatro menos cuarto encima de la pizarra.**

—(C), **coge las seis menos cuarto y dáselas a (D).**

—(E), **coge las siete menos cuarto y dámelas a mí.**

—(F), **ponte las seis y cuarto en la cabeza.**

At this point, fine tune with smaller details such as minutes.

—_____, **pon el reloj a las dos y diez.**

—_____, **ahora son las ocho menos cinco.**

More with the Preterite Tense

Direct a student to act. Then ask another student a question requiring either a short or a long answer in the past tense. Here are some examples.

Be sure the door is open.

—(A), **cierra la puerta y siéntate en la silla.**

Pause.

—(B), **¿qué hizo (A)?**

Answer: "*Cerró la puerta y se sentó en la silla.*"

—(C), **¿cerró (A) los ojos cuando se sentó en la silla?**

Answer: "*No.*"

Writing

Do **Exhibit 9** orally first, eliciting responses from students. Then Distribute **Exhibit 9**. Read each question twice. Then direct students to write responses in the space provided. Finally ask individual students to read the questions followed by the answer they have written.

EXHIBIT 9

1. ¿Qué día es hoy?
2. ¿Qué hora es?
3. ¿Cuál es tu apellido?
4. ¿Cuántos años tienes?
5. ¿Estás casado (-a)?
6. Escribe tu nombre.
7. ¿Eres estudiante?
8. ¿Qué estudias?
9. ¿Es _____ estudiante?
10. ¿Es _____ médico?
11. ¿Está la ventana limpia?
12. ¿Estás enfadado (-a)?
13. ¿Desayunaste? ¿Tomaste café o té?
14. ¿Es _____ alto (-a) o bajo (-a)?
15. ¿Es _____ mecánico?

Pancho Carrancho with the Preterite Tense

Here are some examples you can give to the students before they give you their verbal phrases:

Instructor
- **Pancho Carrancho le dió un puntapié a la puerta.**

Student 1
- **Pancho Carrancho no le dió un puntapié a la puerta; Pancho Carrancho saltó sobre la mesa.**

Student 2
- **Pancho Carrancho no saltó sobre la mesa. Pancho Carrancho comió un bocadillo.**

Student 3
- **Pancho Carrancho no comió un bocadillo. Pacho Carrancho leyó el periódico.**

Student 4
- **Pancho Carrancho no leyó el periódico. Pancho Carrancho escribió una carta.**

Student 5
- **Pancho Carrancho no escribió una carta. Pancho Carrancho cortó flores.**

Then ask the students to give you verbal phrases to write on the board. You begin the game with a declarative sentence about Pancho in the past tense using one of the verbal phrases on the board. The student who gave you that phrase, must immediately negate your sentence, and follow it with a new declarative sentence using another item from the board, and so on.

Class Twenty-Five

Props

a bag of groceries:
- box of rice
- 3 bags of candy
- 2 cans of peas (different brands)
- 2 jars of pickles
- bottle of ketchup
- 2 loaves of bread
- carton of milk
- 6 cans of tuna fish
- 2 boxes of cookies
- banana
- cheese

shopping basket

a pair of scales (for weighing). If you can't find one, pretend the overhead projector is an electronic, computerized scale and treat it as such.)

videos of a supermarket

magazine pictures of foods (glued to stiff cardboard):
- meat cutter cutting meat
- women comparing prices of meat
- bananas
- cheese
- fish
- peas
- cauliflower
- fruit
- vegetables
- meats
- dairy products

Consumer Behavior

Bring to class a bag of groceries (empty cans, boxes and jars with labels and price tags on them will do) as an introduction to the unit on the supermarket. Display the products on your tables around the room, and use your desk as a cash register. Start giving commands while pointing to the right items:

—(A), **coge la caja de arroz y dásela a (B), y dile que lea el precio.**

(Pause)

—(B), **¿cuánto cuesta el arroz?**

Have students play buyer-seller transactions.

—(C), **haz de vendedor.**

Wait for the student to get behind the cash register.

—(D), **camina al mostrador y compra una bolsa de caramelos.**

Pause for the student to that. When s/he has returned to his/her desk, point to the price tag on the candy bag and ask:

—(D), **¿cuánto pagaste por la bolsa de caramelos?**

Contrast

este (-a, -os, -as) / ese (-a, -os, -as) / aquel (aquella, aquellos, aquellas)

Place items at appropriate locations around the classroom, so that space relationships to the speaker indicated by the demonstratives become plain to the students.

—(A), **coge esta barra de pan, pero dale esa barra de pan a** (B).

—_____, **pon aquel bote de pepinillos en tu silla y pon este bote de pepinillos debajo de la mesa.**

—(C), **dale estos caramelos a** (D), **esos caramelos a** (E), **y aquellos caramelos a** (F).

—(F), **dale estas galletas a** (G), **y esas galletas a** (H).

—(I), **pon estas latas de atún en la ventana, esas latas de atún en la pizarra, y aquelllas latas de atún en la cesta.**

A Video of a Supermarket

For production and classroom use of the video, proceed as in the class on the clothing store. Here are some examples of the questions about transactions you can ask.

Pointing to a customer on the screen, ask:

—_____, ¿qué hace este hombre?

Possible answer: "Compra comida."

With a meat cutter on the screen ask:

—_____, ¿qué hace este hombre?

Answer: "Corta carne."

Use this presentation to introduce new verbs.

comparar
- Miren al cliente comparando el precio de dos marcas diferentes de guisantes.

Pause.
- Ahora compara el precio de dos marcas diferentes de salsa de tomate.

Pause.
- Estas señoras comparan los precios de la carne.

pesar
- La dependienta pesa naranjas en esta foto y en la foto siguiente pesa manzanas.

Pause.
- En esta foto el dependiente pesa bananas.

More Food Vocabulary

Have students act with the magazine pictures to indroduce more supermarket vocabulary like food groups:

frutas	**verduras**
carnes	**pescados**
productos lácteos	

Then introduce single foods grouped under those categories, e.g.

carnes:
- **pollo**
- **res**
- **pavo**
- **ternera**
- **cerdo**

Here are some sample commands:

—(A), **coge la foto de la banana y dásela a (B).**

—_____, **pon el queso sobre la ventana.**

—(B), **tírale la banana a (C).**

Role Playing

Role play situations in a supermarket. The instructor plays one role in each situation and a **student plays the other.** Showing the food pictures to the student while you speak, try to have a brief dialogue with the student. For example:

Instructor
- _____, **¿qué quieres de cenar? ¿Te gustaría algo de pescado?**

Student
- **Sí, me gustaría algo de pescado.**

Instructor
- **Bien, escoge el pescado que más te guste y ponlo en la cesta.**

Pause.
- **¿Qué clase de verdura prefieres?**

Student
- **Me gustan la coliflor y los guisantes.**

Class Twenty-Six

Props

TPR Student Kit: The Supermarket©
magazine pictures for items listed in Exhibit 10

Visit to a Local Supermarket

You could take the class to a nearby store to do this lesson. Walk with student around the store and give them shopping commands.

TPR Student Kit: The Supermarket©

Expand the supermarket experience by using this student kit. You can review the food vocabulary and introduce other supermaket products.

Reading

Distribute **Exhibit 10**. Read each item twice. Then individual students will read from the sheet.

EXHIBIT 10
EL SUPERMERCADO

VERBOS

comparar	pesar	costar

Medidas:

1 litro	1 galón	1 libra (lb.)
1/2 litro	1 kilo	1 docena
1/4 litro		

Varios:

los platos	las bolsas de plástico	la caja registradora
la ropa	el carro (de la compra)	el/la cajero (-a)
la balanza	la cesta (de la compra)	el precio

Productos lácteos:

la leche	el queso	el yogurt
la leche desnatada	los huevos	
la leche semidesnatada	la mantequilla	
Comida para el bebé	la nata	
Productos congelados		

Jabón y Artículos de limpieza:

el lavavajillas	el detergente	

Frutas:

el melón	la manzana	el melocotón
la naranja	las uvas	las fresas
la piña	la banana	el limón
la sandía		

Conservas:
    la menestra de verduras   los pepinillos   el cóctel de frutas
    los champiñones en conserva

Charcutería (embutidos):
    las salchichas   el jamón   la mortadela
    el chorizo (la morcilla)   el salchichón   el tocino de panceta

Aves:
    el pollo   el pavo

Pescado:
    el atún   el salmón

Vinos y licores:
    la cerveza   el vino   el whiskey
    el vodka   la ginebra   el ron
    el coñac   el tequila

Verduras y legumbres:
    la lechuga   las habichuelas verdes   el pimiento
    el rábano   los frijoles   el aguacate
    la cebolla   las aceitunas   el pepino
    el tomate   las patatas (fritas)   el maíz
    el apio   la col   el calabacín
    la zanahoria   la coliflor   el arroz
    los guisantes   los champiñones   los garbanzos
    brocoles   los espárragos   las lentenjas
    el ajo

Carnes:
    res   ternera (filete de ...)
    hamburguesa   cordero (chuletas de ...)
    cerdo (chuletas de cerdo)   hígado

Varios:
    el helado   una botella de salsa de tomate
    el pastel   una barra de pan
    las galletas   un cartón de huevos
    una lata de aceitunas   un cartón de leche
    un bote de pepinillos   una bolsa de caramelos
    una tableta de chocolate

ESTRUCTURAS

1. Ella compara los precios.
2. Ella pesa las uvas.
3. Las naranjas están a 58 centavos la libra.
4. Las piñas están a 2,25 dólares cada una.
5. Él pone el cartón de huevos en el carro de la compra.

Class Twenty-Seven

Props

place cards (pictures of places from magazines):
- hospital
- supermarket (bananas)
- post office (envelop, stamps)
- gas station
- bakery
- drug store
- park
- bank
- hairdresser's
- church
- department store
- movie theater
- restaurant
- library
- theater
- airport
- school
- house
- auto repair shop

Introduction of Places

Tape the magazine pictures in several places around the room (walls, windows, closets, board). Then direct students pointing to the right location as places are introduced for the first time. They will walk over where the card is located, and mime the actions stated in the commands. Students should remain at the locations where you sent them until the questions' section is completed. <u>SEND STUDENTS TO PLACES FIRST, JUST TO IDENTIFY LOCATIONS. THEN DO ACTIONS STATED</u>.

—(A), **lleva a (B) al hospital y acuéstalo.**

—(C), **ve al supermercado y compra bananas.**

—(D), **ve a Correos, compra un sello, y echa la carta.**

—(E), **ve a la gasolinera y echa gasolina en el coche.**

—(F), **pon la panadería donde está la farmacia y pon la farmacia donde está la panadería.**

—(G), **ve al parque y juega al béisbol.**

—(H), **ve al banco y saca dinero.**

—(I), **ve a la barbería y córtate el pelo.**

—(J), **ve a la iglesia y habla con el cura.**

—(K) y (L), **vayan a los grandes almacenes.**

Continue until all places are introduced in a sentence. With students remaining at their locations, ask each the following questions:

—(A), **¿dónde estás?**

Answer: "*Estoy en el hospital.*"

—**¿Qué haces en el hospital?**

Answer: "*Estoy acostado.*" OR "*Duermo.*"

—(G), **¿dónde estás?**

Answer: "*Estoy en el parque.*"

—**¿Qué haces?**

Answer: "*Juego al béisbol.*"

—_____, ¿dónde está (J)?

Answer: "Está en la iglesia."
—¿Qué hace?

—*Answer: "Habla con el cura."*

Continue with the rest of the places until each student has had a dialogue with you. Finally ask the whole class with the response expected being a short answer.

—¿Está (D) en Correos?

Answer: "Sí."

—¿Están (K) y (L) en los grandes almacenes?

Answer: "Sí."

After the exercise is completed ask all students to return to their desks and sit down.

Review of the Preterite Tense with Places

Use the exercise on places that you just finished to review the past tense by asking questions. Students will produce long and short responses. Here are some examples:

—_____, ¿fue (A) al hospital?

Answer: "Sí."

—_____, ¿adónde fue (D)?

Answer: "Fue a Correos a echar una carta."

Introduction of the Preterit of "estar"

Continue asking questions now with the verb "**estar**" relating them to the places around the room where you sent the students.

—(A) estuvo en el hospital hace unos minutos. ¿Estuvo (A) en el hospital?

Answer: "Sí."

—¿Estuvo (J) en el hospital?

Answer: "No."

—¿Estuvo (G) en el parque hace unos minutos?

Answer: "Sí."

Reading

After this exercise, copy on the board the following sentences containing familiar verbs written in the past tense and illustrated in a sentence.

Caminó	_____ caminó **a correos ayer.**
Corrí	**Hace unos minutos yo** corrí **a la pizarra.**
Fue	**Ayer** _____ fue al hospital.

Reading Sentences Created by the Students

Ask students to write a sentence in Spanish on a piece of paper that will be turned in to you. Then each individual will dictate his/her sentence to the instructor who will write it on the board. As you write the sentences on the board, correct the vocabulary or the grammar, if neccesary. At the end of the exercise have the students turn their sentences to you. After class, type all of their sentences, and number them; title the exhibit "Sentences Constructed by the Students," and copy or make a transparency for tomorrow's class.

Pancho Carrancho with the Preterite Tense and Vegetables

Follow the same format explained in previous lessons to play this game.

Instructor
- **Pancho Carrnacho se comió el tomate.**

Student A
- **Pancho Carrancho no se comió el tomate; se comió la cebolla.**

Student B
- **Pancho Carancho no se comió la cebolla; se comió la zanahoria."**

And so on.

Class Twenty-Eight

Props

place cards
books
pencils
pens
paper
postcard

Review of Constructed Sentences

Distribute copies of the **Exhibit "Sentences Constructed by the Students"** and have every student read the sentence that s/he wrote. Ask the class:

—¿Quién escribió la frase número uno?

Answer: "Yo."

—Bien, léela.

Go down the list until every student has read his/her sentence. Then ask them to write a new sentence in their notebooks and dictate them to you. Write them on the board.

Review of the Present Indicative and Preterit Tense of the Verbs "ir," "ser" and "estar"

Very quickly fire questions to individual students. The reponse expected is a short answer.

—_____, ¿estuviste aquí ayer?

—(A), ¿fue usted a trabajar ayer?

—_____, ¿estás cansado?

—(C), ¿está sentado (D)?

—¿Es _____ médico?

—¿Qué hora es?

—_____, ¿estás en clase ahora?

—_____, ¿vas al cine los viernes por la noche?

More with Place Cards

This is meant to be a quick review. Start with

- ¿Fuieste a PLACE ayer?,

to review place cards introduced yesterday, and to provide more input for the preterite tense. Point to the appropriate card and ask the students the following questions. Note that the answers given below are only one possibility among many, and students can produce any response that is appropriate. Try to have "real life" dialogues with the students.

Place Card 1

Instructor
- (A), ¿fuiste a la iglesia ayer?

Student A
- Sí.

Instructor
- ¿Por qué?

Student A
- Porque fue domingo.

Place Card 2

Instructor
- (B), ¿Fuiste al banco ayer?

Student B
- No.

Instructor
- ¿Por qué?

Student B
- Porque el banco está cerrado los domingos.

Place Card 3

Instructor
- (C), ¿fuiste a la gasolinera ayer?

Student C
- No.

Instructor
- ¿Por qué?

Student C
- Porque el coche tenía (estaba lleno de) gasolina.

Practice with Ordinal Numbers

—Abre tu libro en la primera página.
—Cierra la primera y la segunda ventana.
—Dale la tarjeta postal a la tercera persona a tu izquierda.
—Dibuja un círculo en el aire con el primer dedo de la mano derecha.

Reading

Distribute **Exhibit 11**. First read each item twice and then each student in turn reads a verbal form from the sheet.

Exhibit 11
EL PRETERITO

1. CAMIN-AR

(Yo)	camin-é
(Tú)	camin-aste
(Usted, él, ella)	camin-ó _____ caminó a Correos ayer.
(Nosotros, -as)	camin-amos
(Ustedes, ellos, -as)	camin-aron

2. COM-ER

com-í   Hace unos minutos comí zanahorias.
com-iste
com-ió
com-imos
com-ieron

3. ESCRIB-IR

escrib-í
escrib-iste
escrib-ió
escrib-imos
escrib-ieron   Ayer los estudiantes escribieron frases en español.

Review of the Preterite

Move one or more students quickly with commands. Then ask the individual(s) involved

—¿Qué hizo usted?
—¿Qué hicieron ustedes?

Or ask someone else by saying

—¿Qué hizo él / ella?

Or

—¿Qué hicieron ellos / as?

Or

—Dinos lo que hicieron ellos/as.

Follow with a role reversal exercise in which students give commands and then ask someone the same questions.

More with the Demonstrative Pronouns

Place pencils, pens, books and pieces of paper at different distances from you; some of them close to you, some at a distance from you, and some far from you. Hold up or point to the appropriate objects just before asking these questions. Students will answer with a short response like: "**Sí.**" "**No.**" or "**Un lápiz.**" "**Lápices,**" and so forth.

—¿Es esto un lápiz?
—¿Qué es eso?

—¿Qué es aquello?
—¿Es esto un libro?
—¿Es aquello un piano?
—¿Es esto una silla?
—¿Son estos libros?
—¿Son esos libros?
—¿Son estos lápices?
—¿Son esos lápices?

Repeat the next three questions pointing alternately to the books, pens, pencils and pieces of papers that are located closer to you, or far from you.

—¿Qué son éstos/as?
—¿Qué son ésos/as?
—¿Qué son aquéllos /as?

Class Twenty-Nine

Props

money
bread
stamps
letters
pencils

place cards
clock
pictures for creating a story (man in hospital; girls at a private Catholic school; barbershop)
more pictures to create stories

Classroom Setup

Place pencils on floor.

Review of the Verb "estar"

Mix commands and questions to practice both the present and the past forms.

—____A____, ve a la pizarra.
—¿Dónde está ____A____?
—____B____, camina a la puerta.
—¿Dónde está ____B____?
Answer: (Cerca de la puerta)
—¿Dónde están los lápices?
Answer: (En el suelo)
—____C____, camina al centro de la clase y canta.
—¿Qué hizo ____C____?
Answer: (Caminó al centro de la clase y cantó)

Pancho Carrancho with Place Cards

Give each student a place card. Have them hold it up so everyone can see it. You begin the game by saying, for example,

Instructor
- Pancho Carrancho estuvo en el parque ayer.

The student who happens to be holding this card has two seconds to retort with, say,

Student A
- No, Pancho Carrancho no estuvo en el parque ayer; estuvo en la escuela.

If the student takes more than two seconds to respond, the person is eliminated and has to put the card down.

Student B
- No, Pancho Carrancho no estuvo en la escuela ayer; estuvo en el taller mecánico.

You keep students on their toes by giving them very little time to reply when their card comes up.

Creating a Story with a Place Card.

Hold up a picture and describe what is in it. Then each student creates a story based on the card you give them. Everyone's story will vary depending upon their picture. Here are a few examples:

—Este hombre está en el hospital. Está acostado pero no está durmiendo. Tiene los ojos abiertos ...

—Estas niñas están en la escuela. Llevan camisas blancas, chaquetas rojas y corbatas negras. Las monjas las miran y hablan con ellas. Esta niña mira una foto...

—Este hombre está en la barbería. Está sentado en el sillón y el barbero le corta el pelo. El barbero sonríe.

Show more pictures and have students create a story about them.

Reading

Distribute **Exhibit 12**. Read each item twice and show the appropriate place card. Also show the appropriate time on your clock after reading the structures telling time.

Exhibit 12

LA CIUDAD
1. Correos (sellos, carta)
2. el banco (dinero)
3. el hospital
4. la farmacia (las medicinas)
5. el supermercado (la comida)
6. la panadería (el pan)
7. el parque
8. la iglesia
9. los grandes almacenes (la ropa)
10. la gasolinera (la gasolina)
11. la escuela
12. la biblioteca
13. la casa
14. la peluquería
15. el aeropuerto
16. el cine
17. el teatro
18. el restaurante
19. el taller mecánico

ESTRUCTURAS

LA HORA

—¿Qué hora es?

—Es la una en punto. (1;00)
Son las cinco y cuarto. (5;15)
Son las cinco y media. (5;30)
Son las seis menos diez. (5;50)
Son las seis y diez. (6;10)

EL PRETERITO DE LOS VERBOS ir Y estar
IR
 fui
 fuiste
 fue   Ayer _____ fue al hospital.
 fuimos
 fueron

ESTAR
 estuve
 estuviste
 estuvo   ¿Estuvo _____ en el parque ayer?
 estuvimos
 estuvieron

Class Thirty

Props

bread	magazine pictures of fast-food restaurant:
paper tablecloth, plates, napkins	cheeseburger
plastic knives, spoons, forks, cups,	shakes or milk
plastic water and wine glasses	french fries
empty salt & pepper shakers	Coke cans
pitcher of water (actually empty)	fried chicken
plastic bottle, bowl, ladle	ice cream cones
writing pad	check tray / tip
pen	2 baseball cups (for student waiters in fast food restaurant)

Classroom Setup

For the formal restaurant, set a table in the middle of the classroom. Have all items listed above ready on a classroom counter or another table to be used as a staging area. Two students will play "waiters," and three will play "customers." You hand the student the items specified in the commands below in order to set the table. When the table is set, the customers will come in and sit at the table. For the fast-food establishment, display the magazine pictures on the board. This way you can have a smooth transition between the two restaurants without having to stop the class. Use your desk as a counter, and the overhead projector to simulate a cash register.

Introduction of Restaurant Vocabulary

Create commands using verbs such as

—poner   —pagar
—pasar   —servir
—derramar   —echar
—pedir

with nouns such as

—el mantel
—el cuchillo
—la cuchara
—el tenedor
—el plato
—el cuenco
—el vaso
—la taza
—el platillo
—la copa
—la jarra
—la botella
—la servilleta
—la sal
—la pimienta
—la cuenta

Start handing out items to the two students posing as waiters, (A) and (B), with commands like:

—Pongamos la mesa.
—Pon el mantel en la mesa.
—Pon los platos en la mesa.
—Toma los cuchillos, los tenedores y las cucharas.
—Pon el cuchillo a la derecha del plato.
—Pon la cuchara junto al cuchillo.
—Pon el tenedor a la izquierda del plato.
—Pon el vaso de agua delante del plato.
—Pon la copa de vino a la derecha del vaso de agua.
—(A), pásale la sal y la pimienta a (B).

At this point the customers can come in.

—(C), (D), y (E), levántense, vayan al restaurante y siéntense a la mesa.
—(B), dale una servilleta a los clientes.

To the customers:

—Desdoblen las servilletas y pónganselas sobre las rodillas.
—(A), ponle a (C) una servilleta al cuello.
—(A), tráele una taza a cada persona.
—(B), Coge la jarra y echa agua en los vasos de los clientes.

No water is actually needed. The student can pretend to be pouring water.

—(C), no derrames la sal en la mesa.

During this first restaurant class, no meal is actually ordered or served. The purpose is to familiarize students with useful restaurant vocabulary. In Class 31, there will more restaurant situations that involve ordering, and serving a full meal.

—(B), sirve la sopa.
—Pásame el pan.
—Pon el platillo debajo de la taza.
—(E), pide la cuenta.
—Paga la cuenta.
—Deja una propina al camarero.

Role playing: A "Fast Food" Establishment

Change the scene now to a humburger establishment. Two students stand behing the counter and take orders. Some other students line up in front of the counter waiting to place their orders. The two employees will write down each order, and run around filling them with the magazine pictures pasted on stiff cardboard. The student behind the counter will simply hand these pictures to the customers. Here is an example of how one of these transactions may go:

Waiter
—¿Qué va a ser?

Customer
—Dos hamburguesas con queso, papas fritas, dos batidos de vainilla, uno grande y otro pequeño, y una Coca-Cola.

Waiter
—De acuerdo.

Customer
—¿Cuánto es?

Waiter
—Nueve dólares, cuarenta y cinco centavos.

Class Thirty-One

Props

same items as for Class Thirty
authentic restaurant menu
plastic play food or pictures from magazines pasted on cardboard
(beer bottle, mineral water, red wine, coffee, milk, tea bag, cake)
paper
tape
books of different colors
calendar for current year

Classroom Setup

For the restaurant section, use the same as for Class Thirty, and either write a menu on the board or distribute printed menus. For the ordinal numbers section, you need to do four things:
1. Number the classroom windows by taping pieces of paper with numbers 1, 2, and 3 written on them.
2. Line up four or five chairs in a row and label them with numbers as well.
3. Lay books of different colors on your desk.
4. Hang up the large calendar on the board.

More Restaurant Role Playing

This time distribute to each student copies of an authentic restaurant menu with pictures of entrees, drinks, salads, vegetables and desserts to order from. Three students, (C), (D), and (E), sit at the table playing customers while others play waiters and cashiers. Have the customers study the menu and make their decisions. Then one of the waiters, (A), will come and take the order. You direct the whole situation with commands beginning with:

—(A), tráeles la carta a los señores.

—Tómale la comanda a los señores.

Pause.

Here is a sampling of how the exchanges may go:

Customer 1
- Para mí, pollo con arroz y una ensalada hortelana.

Customer 2
- Yo prefiero el pescado al horno con verduras y arroz blanco.

Customer 3
- Pimientos rellenos.

Waiter
- ¿Algo de beber?

Customer 1
- Botella de agua mineral sin gas.

Customer 2
- Cerveza.

Customer 3
- Un vino tinto.
— Dale la comanda a (B).

Student B will also play waiter.
— (B), canta la comanda.

Pause.
— (B), tráeles la comida a los señores.

Student B will now ask each customer what they ordered, and serve the food.

Pause.
— Quita los platos de la mesa.

Waiter A
- ¿Desean los señores algo de postre o café?

Customer 1
- Sí por favor, uno con leche.

Customer 2
- Una infusión de té para mí.

Customer 3
- De postre... Una tarta helada, y más agua por favor.

Pause.

Waiter B will now bring and serve dessert, coffee, etc.

Pause.
— (C), pídele la cuenta al camarero.
— (B), trae la cuenta.
— (C), pague la cuenta.
— (B), tráele el cambio al señor.
— (C), Deja una propina en la mesa para el camarero.
— **(B), limpia la mesa.**
— (B), levanta los manteles.

Role Play Restaurant Situations

Have individual students role play situations. Explain the whole situation to the students, or unfold it as you go, whichever you prefer. After you have presented each situation, some volunteers will role play the situation using a few props and simply miming the actions, as you, the instructor, narrate the situation. Students show comprehension of your narration by performing the right actions and showing the right attitudes.

Situation 1
"THE CRAZY WAITER"

A waiter runs around the restaurant like a mad man as he carries a bowl of hot soup in one hand, and a ladle in the other. While playing this acrobatics he spills a bowl of soup in the lap of customer. The customer complains to the manager and demands a new suit. The manager fires the waiter.

Situation 2
"DON'T LEAVE HOME WITHOUT IT"

A customer leisurely reads a newspaper while ordering a five-course meal preceeded by cocktails, appetizers, and followed by coffee, liqueur and cigar. When the check is presented, he discovers that his wallet is missing. The angry restaurant manager does not believe him, and phones the police. Two officers come in and take the customer away.

Ordinal Numbers

Point to window labeled "Number One," and say:

—Lava la primera ventana.

—Ponte de pie delante de la segunda ventana.

—Pega este papel en la tercera ventana y siéntate en la cuarta.

—Escribe el segundo número que yo escriba.

And write two numbers on the board.

—Que estornude el primer estudiante de la tercera fila.

Point to the right student and prompt him to perform the action.

Point to the first book on your desk.

—¿De qué color es el primer libro?

—¿Es el último libro azul?

Point to the calendar.

—¿Es enero o febrero el primer mes del año?

—Señala en el calendario el primero de octubre.

—Abre el calendario en el décimo mes del año.

Everyday Dialogues

Notice how the introduction of informal, "small talk," everyday conversations have being delayed because, although these may look easy for the native speaker, they are grammatically very complex. Interact with students in conversations such as:

Instructor
- Hola (A), ¿cómo estás?

Student A
- Bien gracias, ¿y usted?

Instructor
- Bien gracias. Me alegro de verte en clase. ¿Dónde estuviste ayer? No te vi.

Practice with the Relative Clause

—(A), camina a la persona que está sentada cerca de la puerta y tráela al centro de la sala de clase.

—(B), ¿cómo se llama la persona que (A) trajo al centro de la sala de clase?

—(C), ¿cómo se llama la persona que está sentada junto a ti?

—(D), ven a la pizarra.

Pause.

—(E), dale la mano a la persona que está de pie junto a la pizarra.

Exhibit 12 A

EL RESTAURANTE

VERBOS	VOCABULARIO
pedir (pide)	la comanda
servir (sirve)	la cuenta
tomar la comanda	la propina
pagar (la cuenta)	la sopa
	la sal
	la pimienta
	la servilleta
	el plato
	la ensalada
	el postre

Class Thirty-Two

Review of Everyday Dialogues

For typical social transactions consult **Exhibit 13** and add any other "small talk" conversations you might have had with your students in the previous class. Distribute a copy of the exhibit and read every dialogue twice. Then two students read each dialogue.

Exhibit 13

CHARLA

1. —¡Hola! ¿Qué tal?
   —Regular. Y tú, ¿Cómo estás?
   —Bien, gracias.
   —Hasta luego.
   —Adiós.

2. —Hola, ¿cómo estás?
   —Bien, gracias, ¿y tú?
   —Bien, ¿dónde estuviste ayer?
   —Estuve en casa enfermo.
   —¡Oh! ¡Cuánto lo siento! Me alegro de verte bueno.
   —Gracias.

3. —¡Hola! ¿cómo estás?
   —Muy bien, gracias.
   —Hace un día estupendo. ¿verdad?
   —Sí. ¿Cómo te llamas?
   —Me llamo _____; ¿y tú?
   —_____. Encantado.
   —Igualmente.

5. —ROGELIO: Marta, ésta es mi amiga Carla.
   —CARLA: Mucho gusto.
   —MARTA: Igualmente.

6. —¿Cómo está usted?
   —Estoy un poco cansado. ¿Y tú?
   —Regular.

Quiz 3 (Classes 20-32)

See **Tests** section at the end of the book.

Class Thirty-Three

Props

slides or videotape of a trip you have taken

large world maps (one physical geography, one political geography) or color transparencies

your state's map

objects for description:

plastic lemon	can of soup
hat	tie
key	plate
glass	book

Travelogue

Narrate as you project the slides or show a video, if you made one, of a recent trip you have taken. Students usually enjoy seeing their language instructor in an authentic language setting. Notice that the actual text and questions for your slides or video will, of course, depend on the place you visited and what they show. Sample the effectiveness of communication by asking students to point things out on the screen, or by asking questions like:

—(A), ¿viviste en   NAME OF THE CITY OR TOWN SEEN IN THE VIDEO ?

Pause.

—¿Puedes describir qué tiendas hay en la calle?

—(B), ¿qué es esta escena? ¿Puedes describirla, por favor?

Some Follow-up Geography

Display large maps of the world and your state, or make and show transparencies. Direct students in a geographic exploration with commands and questions.

norte / sur / país

- Señala Norteamerica en el mapa.
- Señala Sudamérica.
- ¿Qué país está situado al sur de los Estados Unidos?
- ¿Qué país está al norte de los Estados Unidos?
- España limita al norte con Francia.
- ¿Qué país está situado al sur de México?
- ¿De dónde eres?
- Muéstranos en el mapa dónde vives ahora.

este / oeste / océano

- El Océano Atlántico está al este de los Estados Unidos.
- Señala el Océano Atlántico.

Pause.

- El océano Pacífico está al oeste de los Estados Unidos.
- Señala el Océano Pacífico.
- España limita al oeste con Portugal.

estado
- ¿Dónde está STATE WHERE YOU ARE TEACHING ?

capital
- ¿Cuál es la capital de STATE WHERE YOU ARE TEACHING ?
- ¿Cuál es la capital de Estados Unidos?
- ¿Cuál es la capital de México / Canadá / Guatemala / Costa Rica / Argentina / Chile / Perú / Ecuador / Bolivia / El Salvador / Colombia / Uruguay / Paraguay / Nicaragua / Venezuela / Honduras / Panamá / Cuba / Puerto Rico / España / Portugal/ Francia / el Reino Unido / Italia / Grecia / Alemania ?

continente
- Los Estados Unidos son un país de Norteamerica.
- América es un continente.
- Señala la capital de los Estados Unidos.
- España está en Europa.
- Europa es un continente.
- Señala la capital de España.

mar
- Señala el mar Mediterráneo.
- Señala el mar del Caribe.
- Señala el mar Negro.

golfo
- Señala el Golfo de México.
- Señala el Golfo Pérsico.

río
- Señala el río más largo de Norteamérica.

Pause.

- Señala el río más largo de Sudamérica.

montaña
- **Señala las montañas más altas de Norteamérica.**
- **Señala las montañas más altas de Sudamérica.**

desierto
- Señala un desierto en Arizona.
- Señala un desierto en Africa.

isla
- Señala la isla de Cuba.
- Irlanda es una isla. Señala Irlanda.
- Señala las Islas Británicas.
- Señalas las Islas Canarias.
- ¿Es Hawaii una isla?

lago
- Señala un lago en Norteamérica.
- Señala un lago en Oregón.

valle

- Señala un valle en California.
- Señala un valle en Oregón.

lenguas

Ask these question as you point to the countries mentioned below on the map.

—¿Se habla inglés en Norteamérica? ¿y en Gran Gretaña?

—¿Hablan inglés en Inglaterra?

—¿Se habla inglés en Sudamérica?

—¿Qué lenguas se hablan en Sudamérica?

—Señala en el mapa algunos países donde se habla inglés.

—Señala en el mapa algunos países donde se habla español.

—¿Se habla español en Brasil?

—Señala en el mapa dónde se habla francés.

Object Description

First you describe some objects as you show them. Then play a game. Have students pick up one from a box containing many objects. Make them hide the object so you don't know what it is. Then you ask questions to figure out what object they picked.

One at a time, give an object to an individual student and ask him or her to describe it. For instance, given a lemon, a student could say:

—Es una fruta. Es un limón y es amarillo.

You can interject with questions like:

—¿Es redondo o cuadrado?

—¿Es suave o áspero?

—¿Es más grande que tu mano?

This exercise could be done blindfolding the sudent and then handing out an object to the student. Given a can of soup, antoher student could come up with something like this:

—Es una lata. Está llena. Es dura.

Continue with other small objects listed under Props above, and other objects in the room. For example, pointing to the board, ask a student:

—Describe la pizarra.

A student could say:

—La pizarra está en la pared de enfrente. Es grande y es un rectángulo. Es de color verde y hay algo escrito con tiza.

Class Thirty-Four

Props

large world map
flags from different countries
family pictures or slides
family tree

Flags

Use flags from different countries to reinforce names of countries

—Dame la bandera de Francia.

—Pon la bandera de los Estados Unidos en la mesa.

—Pásame la bandera de México.

—Pon la bandera de España junto a la bandera del Canadá.

Reading

Prepare and distribute a list of the key lexical items you used during the narration of the travelogue video in Class Thirty-Three. Title it **Exhibit 14: Viajes**. Read the words or structures twice to the students and playback the video again, identifying items on the screen as you read them.

Exhibit 14 (Sample)

VIAJES: VIDEO DE SEVILLA (ESPAÑA)

1. la calle (ancha / estrecha)
2. el río
3. el barco
4. el puente
5. la torre
6. la universidad
7. el autobús
8. el taxi
9. los coches (los automóviles, los carros)
10. los coches de caballos
11. la bicicleta
12. los turistas
13. el árbol (plural: los árboles)
14. las palmeras
15. el parque
16. los pájaros
17. los patos
18. la plaza
19. la catedral
20. el restaurante
21. el camarero
22. la autopista

Distribute also **Exhibit 15: Geography**. Read each item twice and point it out on the map.

EXHIBIT 15
GEOGRAFIA

VOCABULARIO

```
      N
  O  -+-  E
      S
```

el norte
el sur
el este
el oeste
el mapa
el continente
la isla
el río
la montaña
el valle
el desierto
el lago
el golfo
el cabo
la península
la selva
el mar
el océano
el Océano Atlántico
el Océano Pacífico
el Mar Caribe
el Mar Mediterráneo
el Golfo de México
el Golfo Pérsico

el país
el estado
la ciudad
la capital
Norteamérica
Centroamérica
Sudamérica
Europa
Asia
Oceanía (Australia)
Estados Unidos (Washington)
Canadá (Otawa)
Ciudad de México (México, D.F.)

Reino Unido / Inglaterra (Londres)
Francia (París)
Alemania (Berlín)
Italia (Roma)
Grecia (Atenas)
España (Madrid)
Portugal (Lisboa)
Cuba (La Habana)
Guatemala (Guatemala)
Honduras (Tegucigalpa)
Nicaragua (Managua)
Costa Rica (San José)
Panamá (Ciudad de Panamá)
Colombia (Bogotá)
Venezuela (Caracas)
Ecuador (Quito)
El Salvador (San Salvador)
Perú (Lima)
Bolivia (La Paz y Sucre)
Uruguay (Montevideo)
Paraguay (Asunción)
Argentina (Buenos Aires)
Chile (Santiago)
Puerto Rico (San Juan)
República Dominicana (Santo Domingo)

VERBOS

viajar
vivir

ESTRUCTURAS

—¿De dónde eres?
—Soy de _____ .

Family Vocabulary

Draw your family tree on the board or on a transparency. If you like, you can also show a home video of your family or show slides. Refer to the family tree with utterances that establish the relationship of other family members to yourself. Students are usually very interested in knowing about their instructor's family, and can easily identify mother, father, etc. Obviously the text will vary depending on your actual relatives that appear on the family tree. Here is an example of how the narration may go. The blanks in the text stand for names of your family members. Point to the pictures or the slides and the family tree as appropriate.

—Estos son mis padres.
—Este es mi padre, y ésta es mi madre.
—Se llaman _____ y _____.
—Mi padre es (era) el marido (esposo) de mi madre.
—Mi madre es (era) la mujer (esposa) de mi padre.
—Están (estaban) casados.
—Yo soy su hijo.
—Estos son mis abuelos.
—Este es mi abuelo, y ésta es mi abuela.
—Están (estaban) casados.
—Yo soy su nieto.
—Ellos tuvieron muchos nietos.
—Estos son mis hermanos.
—Este es mi hermano, y ésta es mi hermana.
—Tengo (NUMBER) hermanos.
—Mis hermanos se llaman _____, _____, y _____.
—Estos son mis tíos.
—Este es mi tío, y ésta es mi tía.
—Están casados y tienen dos niños.
—Mi tío es el hermano de mi madre (padre).
—Mi tía es la hermana de mi madre (padre).
—Yo soy su sobrino.
—El hijo de mi tío es mi primo.
—La hija de mi tío es mi prima.
—El marido de mi hermana es mi cuñado.
—La mujer de mi hermano es mi cuñada. Esta es mi cuñada.
—Esta es mi mujer (esposa).
—Este es mi marido (esposa)
—Los padres de mi esposa son mis suegros.
—Este es mi suegro y ésta es mi suegra.
—Yo soy su yerno.
—Estos son mis hijos (niños).
—Yo tengo dos niños. Se llaman _____ y _____.
—Señala a mi padre.
—¿Cómo se llama(ba)?
—Señala a mi hermano.
—Señala mis tíos.
—Señala el marido de mi tía.
—¿Cómo se llaman mis primos?
—¿Cómo se llama mi tía?

Before ending the class, remember to ask each student to bring two or three family pictures for tomorrow's class.

Family Tree

Have students draw their family tree. Ask them to identify their family members for the class using the tree.

Class Thirty-Five

Props

students' family pictures
book
wedding invitation as model
black hat for groom
bouquet of white flowers for bride

Classroom Setup

Arrange chairs and other classroom furniture to resemble a church.

Family Vocabulary

Have a conversation with each student using two family pictures as referents. Here is a sample of the questions and commands to be used. Point to a person in one of the pictures and ask:

—¿Quién es éste?

—¿Es éste tu hermano?

—¿Es ésta tu hermana?

—¿Es éste tu hijo?

—¿Es ésta tu hija?

—Por favor, señala a tu hermana / madre / padre.

Next instruct students to point to a family member and give a description of that person.

A Class Wedding

Divide your students into families, and have them introduce themselves to the rest of the class establishing their relationships to one another. Then have a wedding between two people from different families. Once the bride and the groom are selected, present an authentic wedding invitation from a Spanish speaking country. Ask questions on the invitation like

—¿Quién se casa?

—¿Quién es el novio?

—¿Quién es la novia?

—¿Cómo se llaman los padres del novio?

—¿Cómo se llaman los padres de la novia?

—¿Cuándo es la boda?

—¿A qué hora?

—¿Dónde?

Once the students are familiar with the style and format, have them design their own **wedding invitation**.

Next, hand the black hat to the groom and the bouquet of flowers to the student who will play the bride. You can officiate as the minister during the ceremony. You and your students will have great fun with this activity!.

Introduction of Future Constructions

The strategy is to tell what action will occur, and then students will see the event happen as you perform the action.
> —**Voy a escribir en la pizarra.**

Then write something on the board.
> —**Voy a abrir mi libro.**

And open your book.
> —**Voy a leer una frase del libro.**

And read a sentence from the book.
> —(A), **vas a contarte los dedos, y después vas a señalar a (B) con el primer dedo.**

(A) will then execute the chain of behavior.
> —**Voy a sentarme en la silla y voy a leer mi libro.**
> —**Voy a ir a la pizarra y voy a dibujar un círculo.**
> —**Ahora voy a ir a la mesa.**
> —(A), **en un minuto vas a ponerte de pie, y vas a meterte la mano en el bolsillo.**
> —(B), **en un momento vas a salir de la clase y vas a beber agua.**
> —(C), **en un momento vas a apagar la luz, y después vas a golpear la pared tres veces.**

Before the student begins performing these actions, ask him/her promptly:
> —(C), **¿qué vas a hacer?**
> Answer: *"Voy a apagar la luz y golpear la pared tres veces."*

The student will then proceed to do this. After © completes the action, ask:
> —(D), **¿qué hizo (C)?**
> Answer: *"Apagó la luz y golpeó la pared tres veces."*

As in the last example, emphasize the future constructions but intermix other tenses like the preterit and the present indicative until students respond with flexibility to rapid shifts in verb tenses. To review the present indicative, while an action is in progress, ask a question using this tense.
> —(A), **camina a la mesa de (B) a ver la foto de su madre.**

While (A) is doing this, ask:
> —(A), **¿qué haces?**

To which (A) student can answer:
> —**Camino a la mesa de (B) a ver la foto de su madre.**

Now cue a future action by saying:
> —(A) **y** (B) **van a caminar al centro de la clase.**

Then before the action takes place, ask the class:
> —**¿Qué van a hacer ellos?**

Future Imbedded in the Conditional

After this, use another format by embedding the future construction in the conditional.
> —**Si yo camino al centro de la clase, (A) se va poner de pie en su silla.**

Walk to the center of the room, and look expectantly to (A) for him/her to stand up. Now you can expand the format to make what will happen contingent upon a decision by a designated student:
> —**Si (A) camina al centro de la clase, (B) se va a poner de pie en su silla, pero si (A) dibuja una cara feliz en la pizarra, (B) la va a borrar.**

Class Thirty-Six

Props

broom	dishes (platos)
plastic plants	Coke
duster	toy house
mop	TPR Student Kit: The Home©
phone	(teacher transparency)
small rug	TPR Student Kit: The Kitchen©
	(teacher transparency)

Classroom Setup

Set up sofa.

Review of Family Vocabulary

By now students have internalized vocabulary like **madre, padre, hermano, hermana, abuelo, abuela, hijo, hija.** Distribute a copy of **Exhibit 16: La familia** to each student. Read each item twice; then individual students read a vocabulary item and use it in a sentence.

Exhibit 16

LA FAMILIA

el marido (el esposo), la mujer (la esposa), los esposos
el padre, la madre, los padres
el hijo, la hija, los hijos
el hermano, la hermana, los hermanos
el abuelo, la abuela, los abuelos
el nieto, la nieta, los nietos
el tío, la tía, los tíos
el sobrino, la sobrina, los sobrinos
el primo, la prima, los primos
el suegro, la suegra, los suegros
el yerno, la nuera, los hijos políticos
el cuñado, la cuñada, los cuñados

New Commands: The Home

To do the following command, hand a student the broom or have him pretend to sweep the floor with appropriate hand movements.

barre
- Coge la escoba y barre el suelo.

limpia
- Coge la fregona y limpia el suelo.

pasa
- Pasa la aspiradora.

llama
- Llama a la puerta.

toca el timbre
- Toca el timbre.

The student can mime the previous action with hand movements and making the appropriate sound (ding-dong) at the same time.

—Mira cómo voy a la puerta y toco el timbre.

Then use the new vocabulary in the context of the future.

—En un momento, ____A____ va a barrer el suelo.
—¿Va a cortarse el pelo ____A____?
—(Answer: "No. Va a barrer el suelo.)

TPR Student Kits:
The Home, the Kitchen; The Toy House

Use these two kits to introduce the house vocabulary. If you don't have the kits, the alternatives are either to take the class to your home, or have the students mimic the actions in class. Here is a selective vocabulary list. You will find a complete list in Exhibit 17. Introduce the first basic 5 items in the list

sala de estar`	dormitorio
cuarto de baño	cocina
comedor	

Then:

mesa	silla
cama	sofá
armario	cajón
frigorífico	aspiradora
alfombra	plumero
maceta	

Combine above items and others in expressions like these. Mime actions.

pon la mesa
haz la cama
pásale la aspiradora a la alfombra
riega las flores
quita el polvo
siéntate en el sofá y descansa
lava los platos
llama por teléfono
contesta el teléfono
ve al cuarto de baño y dúchate
abre el frigorífico y coge una Coca-Cola

Class Thirty-Seven

Props

place cards (see Props for Class 27)
house chores video

Verb Flash Cards:

One verb per card. Use verbs students are already familiar with. Here are some you can use:

golpear	cerrar	coger	salir	beber
bailar	cortar	estar	ir	sentarse
caminar	dormir	hablar	echar	dibujar
cantar	hacer	vender	estudiar	barrer
borrar	romper	dar	abrir	pasar
correr	escribir	leer	ver	pesar
sonreír	comprar	quitarse	limpiar	comparar
lavar	tocar	ver	levantarse	ser
poner	saltar		mirar	

Review of Future Construction

Ask question about future events. Students invent possible answers.

> (A) va a tocar el timbre.
> —¿Qué va a hacer (A)?
> —¿Qué va a tocar (A)?
> —¿Quién va tocar el timbre?
> —¿Va (A) a tocar el timbre?

More Practice with Future Construction: Pancho Carrancho with Verb Cards

Play this word game as usual. Write on the board all verbs listed under Props. These should be exactly the same verbs printed on the flash cards. At random, hand out a flash card to each student with a verb written on it; they should hold up the card so everyone can see it. Eliminate students who take more than two or three seconds to react to your statement, by crossing out their verb on the board. You begin with say:

Instructor
- Pancho Carrancho **va a tocar el timbre.**

Then the student who happens to be holding the card with the verb "tocar" on it, immediately responds with:

Student A
- **No, Pancho Carrancho no va a tocar el timbre;**

and invents a new sentence, like
- **va a mirar a las chicas.**

If the student fails to react with a "no" within two seconds, cross his/her verb out, and provide another sentence choosing another verb from the board. For example:
Instructor
- Pancho Carrancho **va a lavar los platos.**

The student holding the card "lavar" will come in promptly with a "no", and then will invent another sentence in the future by selecting another verb from the list that is no yet crossed out. Of course, students choosing transitive verbs will need to provide an object to make a meaningful sentence. The game may continue in this fashion:
Student B
- No, Pancho Carrancho **no va a lavar los platos; va a golpear al maestro en el hombro.**

Student C
- No, Pancho Carrancho **no va a golpear al maestro en el hombro; va a borrar la pizarra.**

Student D
- No, Pancho Carrancho **no va a borrar la pizarra; va a lavar la ropa.**

Student E
- No, Pancho Carrancho **no va a lavar la ropa; va a poner la mano en la mesa.**

Student F
- No, Pancho Carrancho **no va a poner la mano en la mesa; va a cerrar la puerta.**

Student G
- No, Pancho Carrancho **no va cerrar la puerta; va a cortar pan.**

An so on. If students are having trouble, you may add objects or prepositional phrases to the verb cards to make it easier for them. Thus, you can print on the cards meaningful phrases like:

hacer la comida	vender su coche	tomar café
romper la botella	dar dinero a la escuela	cortar el pan
ir de compras	quitarse los pantalones	barrer el suelo
ir a San Francisco	mirar la televisión	pasar la aspiradora a la alfombra
comprar en el supermercado	echar agua en el vaso	pesar las naranjas
tocar la pared	abrir el libro	comparar el precio de dos marcas diferentes de guisantes
coger el lápiz	ser ingeniero	
ser feliz hoy	limpiar su cuarto	

Future with Place Cards

Give each student a card with a different place on it. If there are not enough cards for everyone, two students can share a card. They should hold up the card for everyone to be able to see it. Then ask a question about a future event, and the student(s) will answer making a reference to the place in the card that he (they) is (are) holding. For example:

—(A), ¿adónde vas a ir?

Answer: "**Voy a ir a Correos.**"

—(B), ¿adónde van a ir usted y (C)?

Answer: "**Vamos a ir al parque.**"

—(C), ¿adónde va a ir (D)?

Answer: "**A casa.**"

Class Thirty-Eight

Props

pictures from magazine for home items listed in Exhibit 17
video of house chores
TPR Student Kit: The Home®   TPR Student Kit: The Kitchen®

Role Reversal

Ask a student to teach part of the class today by reading one of the lessons out of the TPR Kits: The Home or The Kitchen. Other students can perform the commands using the kits, and answer the questions, if any.

Reviewing

Distribute copies of **Exhibit 17: La casa** which contains all the vocabulary internalized in class about the home. Use either transparencies of the pictorial exhibits, magazine pictures, the transparecies included in the TPR Student Kits, or all three to identify each item as you read it a couple of times.

Exhibit 17

LA CASA

El dormitorio	El cuarto de baño
la cama	el lavabo
la mesita de noche	la bañera
el despertador	la ducha
la almohada	el espejo
la silla	el váter, el inodoro
la cómoda	las toallas
el cajón	el jabón
	el papel higiénico
	el secador

El cuarto de los niños	El comedor
el ropero	la mesa del comedor
el espejo	el aparador
	la lámpara
	las velas
	las sillas

La sala de estar	La cocina
el sofá	el fregadero
el sillón	la cocina de gas
la alfombra	la mesa de cocina
el escritorio	la despensa
la estantería de libros	el horno
la mesita de centro	el frigorífico

el televisor
la radio
el tocadiscos, el estéreo
el cuadro
la cortina
el teléfono
la lámpara

El patio / el jardín
el árbol
la piscina
las macetas de flores
el cubo de la basura
la lavadora
la secadora
el cubo

el congelador
el hielo
las ollas, los pucheros
la cacerolas, los cazos
la sartén (-es)
el grifo
la batidora
el horno de microondas
las toallas de papel
el lavaplatos
la cafetera
la tetera

El garaje / el lavadero
la escoba
la fregona
la aspiradora
la bicicleta

ESTRUCTURAS
1. Llama a la puerta.
2. Toca el timbre
3. Contesta el teléfono.
4. Barre el suelo con la escoba.
5. Limpia el suelo con la fregona.
6. Pásale la aspiradora a la alfombra.
7. Haz la cama.
8. Lava los platos.
9. El horno está caliente.
10. El congelador está frío.

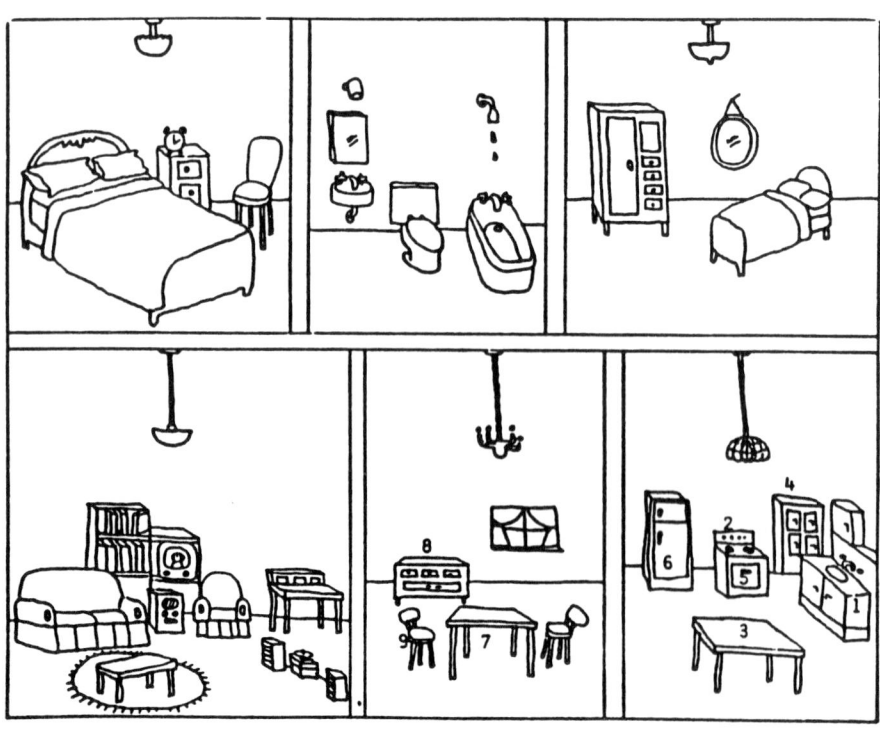

Class Thirty-Nine

Props

picture from magazine showing models with different types of clothes
large box
white plate
kleenex
vase
chalk
book
napkin
glass
magazine
silk scarves of different colors
tie
plastic lemon

Costumes

You should consider dressing up today in black tie, as a magician, for the Introduction of the "hay" section.

Clothes Review

Show different pictures with models wearing clothes and ask the students each time:

—(A), ¿qué ropa lleva?

—¿Te pondrías tú esta ropa?

—¿Te has puesto algo así antes?

Home Review

Ask students to tell about household chores that they do or someone else does at home. Give them some examples like:

—Tenemos una aspiradora. Yo le paso la aspiradora a la alfombra.

—Barro el suelo con la escoba.

—Mi padre hace el fregado (lava los platos).

—Yo pongo y saco los platos y cubiertos del lavaplatos.

—Yo saco la basura a la calle.

—Mi hermana le quita el polvo a los muebles.

—Mi madre limpia el suelo de la cocina.

—_____ lava los cristales de las ventanas.

—_____ limpia el cuarto de baño.

Introduction of "hay"

Place the box on the table. If you like, you can lend this exercise the atmosphere of a magic show by first showing the box empty, inside out. Next perform some "magic trick," and, all of a sudden, the box is full of things. Start to take them out. Although everything you are going to do is routinely take out one object after another from a box, try to play up the element of suspense, as if, in just a moment, your blue silk scarf were about to turn into a white rabbit.

Be sure the objects mentioned here are properly placed before you begin the exercise. Students will listen to you, and answer yes or no to your questions having "hay" as a constituent, when that is called for.

—En esta caja hay un pañuelo azul.
—Y un pañuelo blanco.
—Y un pañuelo rojo.
—En esta caja hay un plato blanco.

Take out the plate and show it to the class.

—En mi bolsillo hay un pañuelo de papel.

And take out the kleenex.

—En este jarrón hay un poco de agua.

And shake the vase to hear the water.

—¿Hay una tiza en el suelo?
Answer: "Sí."
—¿Hay un cuchillo en el plato?
Answer: "No."
—¿Hay un frigorífico en la sala de clase?
Answer: "Sí / No."

Continue asking questions that now require a longer answer:

—¿Hay un libro o una tiza en el suelo?
Answer: "Una tiza."
—¿Hay un estudiante alto en esta clase?
Answer: "Sí."
—¿Quién es?
Answer: "_____; él / ella es muy alto (-a).
—¿Hay un médico en la sala?
Answer: "Sí _____ es médico." OR "No."

Place the box on the table, a book under the box, and a napkin next to it.

—En la mesa hay una caja.
—Debajo de la caja hay un libro.
—Junto a la caja hay una servilleta.

From this point on, start taking out the objects inside the box as you mention them.

—En la caja hay una corbata ... y un vaso .... y una revista ... y un limón ...

Continue with a series of questions to which students are expected to answer yes or no.

—¿Hay una caja en la mesa?
—¿Hay una tiza en la caja?

Next cue with an example to show that you want an expanded response to each question.

—¿Hay una caja o una revista en la mesa?
Answer: "Hay una caja en la mesa."
—¿Qué más hay en la mesa?
Possible answer: "En la mesa hay un vaso?
—¿Qué más?
Possible answer: "Hay una revista, un libro, plato, una sevilleta, un pañuelo rojo, un pañuelo blanco ..."

And so on.

Describe Yourself: Adjectives

Write a list of descriptive words on the board, and their opposites, if they exist, next to them. Also show pictures if you can.

LIST OF ADJECTIVES
rubio / moreno
alto / bajo
trabajador / perezoso
bueno / malo
amable
agradable / desagradable
simpático / antipático
amistoso
guapo / feo
bonito / feo
inteligente / torpe
listo / tonto
rico / pobre

Also include some nouns like

LIST OF NOUNS
hombre / mujer
estudiante / profesor
ama de casa
abogado
policía
médico, etc.

Each student will describe himself/herself in three sentences using these words. Descriptions, naturally, don't have to be true to fact, and students can just pick whatever adjectives they like. Cue them by describing yourself first. For example:

—Soy hombre. Soy profesor. Soy simpático.

Students will continue with their own descriptions. For instance:

Student A
- Soy estudiante. Soy inteligente. Soy bonita.

Student B
- Soy alta. Soy amistosa. Soy buena.

Class Forty

Props

umbrella	expensive pen (coat)	(weight lifter, muscle builder)
rock	cheap pen (coat)	pictures of fur coats, gold watches, expensive cigarette lighters, fountain pens (for adjective "caro')
bread	picture of fat girl	
pillow	picture of fat boy	
sponge	picture of thin girl	cheap pen, cheap cigarette lighter (for adjective "barato")
world map	picture of thin boy	
bottle of beer	picture of an old man	pictures of old car / new car
ice cube tray	picture of an old woman	picutres of hot / cold weather
one thick book	picture of a young man	pictures of refrigerator and stove (for 'frío'/ 'caliente')
one thin book	picture of a young woman	
one old book		new alarm clock / old alarm clock
one new book (light paperback)	picture of a weak man	easy arithmetic flash card (for adjective 'fácil')
	picture of a strong man	hard arithmetic flash card (for adjective 'difícil')
		pictures of rich boy / poor boy

Classroom Setup

Display the objects listed above on your desk, and the pictures on the board. There should be a wall clock on the wall. Place one chair near a student, and another chair far from him. One heavy chair, and one light chair next to you.

Review of "hay"

Make the review fast moving with questions like:

> ¿Hay un frigorífico en la clase?
> ¿Hay un reloj en la pared?
> ¿Hay hombres y mujeres en esta clase?
> ¿Hay coches en la clase?
> ¿Hay cortinas (o persianas) en las ventanas?
> ¿Hay un paraguas en la mesa?
> ¿Hay un hombre alto y una mujer baja en la clase?
> ¿Hay personas y gatos en la clase?

Reviewing: Exhibit 18 (future time; structure "hay").

Read each sentence. Then have each student read a sentence which is a review of the immediate future construction, and the structure "hay".

Exhibit 18
EL FUTURO INMEDIATO
ir + a + verb in the infinitive

(Yo)	voy a dormir	(Nosotros, -as)	vamos a dormir
(Tú)	vas a dormir	(Ustedes)	van a dormir
(Usted, él, ella)	va a dormir	(Ellos, -as)	van
(Yo)	no voy a dormir	(Nosotros, -as)	no vamos a dormir
(Tú)	no vas a dormir	(Ustedes)	no van a dormir
(Usted, él, ella)	no va a dormir	(Ellos, -as)	no van a dormir

¿Voy a dormir? ¿Vamos a dormir?
¿Vas a dormir? ¿Van a dormir?
¿Va a dormir? ¿Van a dormir?

ESTRUCTURAS: hay

Hay una pluma en el suelo.
Hay libros en la mesa.
No hay un frigorífico en la sala de clase.
No hay cortinas en las ventanas.
¿Hay un piano en la sala de clase?
¿Hay muchas chicas en esta clase?

Review of poder

Use "poder" in a sentence, then demonstrate.

—Yo puedo tocarme la nariz. Miren.
—Yo puedo darle la mano a _____. Miren.
—Yo puedo levantar esta silla con una mano y ponerla en la mesa. Miren.
—¿Puedes levantar esta silla _____? (Pause)
—Pues hazlo. A ver.
—Yo puedo tocarme los pies manteniendo las piernas rectas. Miren.
—¿Puedes tocarte los pies manteniendo las piernas rectas? (Pause)
—A ver. Hazlo.
—¿Puedes tocar el suelo manteniendo las piernas rectas?
—Yo puedo escribir con la mano izquierda. Miren.
—¿Puedes escribir con la mano izquierda?

More with Opposites

alto / bajo
- Dibuja una montaña alta.

cerca / lejos
- _____, camina a la silla que está cerca de ti, pero corre a la silla que está lejos de ti.
- Sacramento está cerca de San Francisco, pero Nueva York está lejos de San Francisco.

gordo / delgado
- Coge la foto del muchacho(a) gordo (a) y ponla junto a la foto del muchacho(a) delgado (a).
- Dame la foto de la muchacha delgada.
- Dibuja un hombre gordo.
- Dibuja un hombre delgado.
- Coge el libro gordo y dámelo.
- Coge el libro delgado y tíraselo a _____.

pesado / ligero
- Este libro es muy pesado.
- Este libro es muy ligero. Es poco pesado.
- Tírale el libro ligero a _____.
- Esta silla es muy pesada.
- Esta silla es ligera. Pesa poco.

viejo / joven
- Busca la foto del hombre viejo y la mujer vieja, y dáselas las dos a _____.
- Toca la foto de la mujer joven.

viejo / nuevo
- Pon el libro nuevo debajo del libro viejo.
- Dame el despertador nuevo.
- Pon el despertador viejo a las siete.
- Toca la foto del coche nuevo.
- Toca la foto del coche viejo.

fuerte / débil
- Pon la foto del hombre fuerte delante del hombre débil.

blando / duro
- La almohada es blanda.
- La piedra es dura.
- El pan está duro.
- La esponja es blanda.

Show arithmetic flashcards for "easy" and "difficult."
fácil / difícil
- Esto es fácil.
- Esto es difícil.
- Ahora señala las matemáticas difíciles.

estrecho / ancho
- Dibuja una calle estrecha en la pizarra.
- Ahora, dibuja una calle ancha.
- En el mapa, señala un país ancho.
- Ahora señala un país estrecho.

frío / caliente
- Señala el frigorífico y la cocina de gas.
- El frigorífico está frío.
- La cocina de gas está caliente.
- Dame una botella de cerveza fría.

Show the ice cube tray.
- El hielo está frío. Toca el hielo.

Show pictures for the next two commands.
- Hace frío.
- Hace calor.

Make a gesture to signify "cold" and ask Student A:
- (A), ¿tienes frío?

Make a gesture to signify "hot" and ask Student B:
- (B), ¿tienes calor?

caro / barato
- Esta pluma es muy cara.
- Escribe con la pluma cara, pero no la pierdas.
- Esta pluma es muy barata. Escribe con ella.
- Este reloj es muy caro. Es de oro.
- Este reloj es muy barato. Es de plástico.
- Este abrigo es muy caro. Es de piel.
- Este encendedor es muy caro.
- Este encendedor es muy barato.

rico / pobre

Show picture of rich, famous man.
- Este hombre es muy rico. Tiene mucho dinero, muchos hoteles, y casinos y casas y coches.
- Este niño es pobre. No tiene casa, ni ropa, ni dinero, ni familia.

Class Forty-One

Props

objects and pictures for opposites (See Props for Classes 9, 16 and 40)
picture or transparencies of car (the outside and the inside of the car, driver's panel)

Review of Opposites

Use the imperative to review both the pairs of opposites introduced in Class Forty, and those the students that were introduced in Class Nine and Class Sixteen. Distribute **Exhibit 19: Review of Contrasts**.

Exhibit 19
REVIEW OF CONTRASTS

abierto (a) / cerrado (a)	grande / pequeño	fuerte / débil
recto (a) / curvo (a)	lleno / vacío	blando / duro
derecho / izquierdo	claro / oscuro	fácil / difícil
largo / corto	sucio / limpio	ancho / estrecho
feliz / triste	cerca / lejos	frío / caliente
alto (a) / bajo (a)	delgado (a) / gordo (a)	caro / barato
mojado / seco	joven / viejo (a)	pesado / ligero
guapo (a) (bonito (a)) / feo (a)	nuevo / viejo	rico / pobre

Introduction of "no puedo ... porque ..."

Since students have already internalized the meaning of "puedo," the transition to "no puedo" should be smooth. Begin with statements like:

—No puedo tocar el techo porque está muy alto.

Get on your toes, and reach for the ceiling with your hand.

—No puedo levantar la mesa porque es muy pesada.

And try to lift your desk. Pretend to make a big effort to no avail.

—No puedo tirar esta silla porque es demasiado pesada.

Show dramatically that it is impossible for you to throw a chair.

Now ask questions to students.

—¿Puedes tocar el techo?
Answer: "No, no puedo."
—¿Por qué no puedes tocar el techo?
Answer: "Porque está muy alto."
—¿Qué cosas no puedes tocar?
Answers will vary: "*El techo, la luz, la parte de arriba de la ventana, el reloj.*"
—(A), ponte derecho; dobla el cuerpo.
—(A), ¿puedes tocarte los pies sin doblar las piernas (con las piernas rectas)?

And try to do this yourself to show the student what you mean.

Pause.

Keeping the same position, ask the student:
—¿**Puedes tocar el suelo?**

Pause, and have the student try.

An Imaginary Car

To teach how to drive the car, sit in a row with students to your left and right. Each person sits on a chair with enough space to move their arms and legs. Each movement of the feet and arms should look like a chorus line. You can teach a manual transmission car or an automatic.

After you identify brakes, accelerator, gear shift, and give commands like "**conduce**," "**para**," etc. simulate an imaginary sedan by arranging two chairs behind two other chairs facing the class. You could also use a toy car of the type that toddlers use, or somethig big enough for a person to get inside. Also arrange desks and chairs to set up a gas station. Then direct students with commands. Students should mime all the actions as if they were in a real car. They can also provide sound effects to the execution of certain commands below. Although the imaginary car remains stationary, passengers should make appropriate body movements to create the sensation of motion. They can also wave if they like, or fight in the back seat as children often do.

Ask for four volunteers, and start the command sequence.
—Abran las puertas y suban al coche.

Make sure students lower their head when entering the car, and open doors correctly.
—Abróchense los cinturones.
—Abran las ventanillas.
—¿Quién es el conductor?
—(A), pon la llave y arranca el coche.

Pause.
—Suelta el freno de mano.
—Mete la primera y pon el coche en marcha.
—Vamos a dar un paseo. Adelante.
—Todo seguido. Recto.
—Vuelve a la derecha.

Make sure the driver turns the imaginary steering wheel to the right.
—Todo seguido. Recto.
—Vuelve a la izquierda.
—Pon la radio.

Someone inside the car should start humming a tune.
—Para.
—Apaga la radio.
—Desabróchense los cinturones.
—Suban las ventanillas.
—Abran las puertas.
—Salgan todos.
—Echen el seguro y cierren las puertas.
—(A) cierra tu puerta con llave.

Ask another group of four students to get ready to take over the car.
—(A), abre la puerta del coche.

—(B), (C), y (D) suban al coche también.
—Siéntate al volante.
—Cierra la puerta.
—(A), Pon la llave y arranca el motor.
—Pon el coche en marcha y adelante.
—Echa el intermitente y vuelve a la izquierda.
—Ahora, todo recto.
—(B), dile a (A) que pare en el supermercado.
—(C), dile a (A) que no pare en el supermercado, sino que vaya a los grandes almacenes.
—Echa el freno.
—(A), dile a todos que se callen.

Student A
- Cállense.

—Ahora conduce a la gasolinera.
—Para el coche y apaga el motor.

Role Play a Gas Station Transaction

You can play the attendant and a student plays the driver in an imaginary car. You will need to mime all the actions involved. Direct and ask questions to the driver. Here is a sample of how the verbal interaction may go:

Attendant
- ¿En qué puedo servirle?

Driver
- Póngame gasolina.

Attendant
- ¿Se lo lleno?

Driver
- Sí.

Place yourself at the right location and mime the action of filling up the tank holding a pump in your hand.
Attendant

Pointing to the hood.
- ¿Quiere que le mire el aceite?

Driver
- Sí, por favor.

Raise the hood and mime checking the oil level.
Driver
- Examine la presión de los neumáticos.

Go around the car checking all four tires.
- Por favor, limpie el parabrisa mientras voy a los servicios.

Pause.
Attendant
- Por favor, abra el portaequipajes, necesito sacar la rueda de repuesto. Voy a cambiar la rueda.

Show the Driver the location of the trunk at the back of the car.

Reading

Distribute **Exhibit 20: el coche.** Get pictures or transparencies of a car, both showing the outside and the inside. You will need a good picture of the driver's panel for students to point things out as you read items from the exhibit.

Do orally first before distributing the exhibit. Read each item twice. Next class, give a copy to each student, and review the car vocabulary again.

Exhibit 20

EL COCHE (EL CARRO)

el volante
el cambio de marchas
las marchas (primera, segunda, tercerca, cuarta, punto muerto, marcha atrás)
el freno de mano
el acelerador
el freno
el embrague
el intermitente
la radio
la llave de contacto
el cinturón de seguridad
las luces
el motor
el portaequipajes
el asiento
el capó
la llanta
la rueda
la rueda de repuesto
el conductor
el parabrisas
el limpiaparabrisas
el espejo retrovisor
la puerta
el asiento

TPR Student Kit: The Gas Station©

Use this kit to expand the gas station experience within the classroom.

Class Forty-Two

Props

kitchen: can of Coke, glass
bank: ckeckbook, dollar bills
department store: two or three pairs of pants, shirts, jackets

Classroom Setup

Use clasrrom funiture to set up different playing spaces to act out the situations described below: a car, a kitchen, a bank, a department store, and a bus. Use two parallel columns of chairs to represent the seats of a bus.

Situations

These situations will work better if you read them, and students perform the actions. However, the situations could also be used to practice reading. A student will read and others will perform. Students can mime the actions without actual props. However, it helps to have some objects to set the action and give it some sense of reality. Select different students to play different roles.

These exercises are also good for preparing students for the Final Skit. These sketches are good examples of the type of work they will be creating for the final exam.

Situation 1: Al volante

—Levántate.
—Camina al coche.
—Saca las llaves.
—Abre la puerta.
—Sube.
—Pon la llave de contacto.
—Pon el pie en el acelerador.
—Arranca el coche.
—Suelta el freno.
—Conduce el coche.
—¡Para!
—¡Adelante!
—Semáforo en amarillo. Despacio.
—Semáforo en rojo. Para.
—Espera que cambie el semáforo.
—Conduce el coche otra vez.
—Echa el intermitente para volver a la izquierda.
—Vuelve a la izquierda.
—Echa el intermitente para volver a la derecha.
—Vuelve a la derecha.
—Mira el espejo retrovisor.
—Desvíate a un lado de la carretera.
—Para.
—Apaga el motor.
—Quita la llave.
—Abre la puerta.
—Sal fuera.
—Cierra la puerta.

Situation 2: En la cocina

—Levántate.
—Ve a la cocina.
—Abre el frigorífico.
—Saca una lata de Coca-Cola.
—Cierra el frigorífico.
—Camina al armario.
—Abre el armario.
—Saca un vaso.
—Cierra el armario.
—Camina a la mesa.
—Deja el vaso sobre la mesa.
—Abre la lata.
—Echa Coca-Cola en el vaso.
—Deja la lata sobre la mesa.
—Coge el vaso.
—Camina a la silla.
—Coge la silla, ponla junto a la mesa, y siéntate.
—Bebe un poco de Coca-Cola.
—Descansa.

Situation 3: En el banco

One student plays the teller behind your desk, while others, playing customers, wait in line.

—Ve al banco.
—Abre la puerta.
—Ponte en cola.
—Da un paso adelante.
—Da otro paso más.
—Camina al mostrador.
—Dale un cheque al cajero.
—Di: "Quisiera cobrar este cheque."
—Coge tu dinero.
—Camina a la puerta.
—Abre la puerta y camina a tu coche.

Situation 4: De compras

One student plays the salesperson and another plays the customer in a department store.

—Ve a la tienda.
—Abre la puerta y entra.
—Vendedor, pregunta: "¿En qué puedo servirle?"
—Responde: "Gracias. Sólo estoy mirando."
—Camina y mira por toda la tienda.
—Párate enfrente de los pantalones.
—Coge un par de pantalones.
—Míralos.
—Déjalos.
—Ve a la puerta.
—Abrela y sal fuera.

Situation 5: En el autobús

A student will play the driver seating at a seat in front of the bus. Some studetns are already inside the bus sitting at their seats. Other students wait in line at a bus stop before getting on the bus.

—Levántate.
—Ve a la puerta de la casa.
—Abre la puerta.
—Sal fuera.
—Cierra la puerta.
—Camina a la parada del autobús.
—Espera el autobús.
—Sube.
—Pon el dinero en la caja.
—Busca un asiento libre. Camina al asiento y siéntate.
—Mira por la ventana.
—¿Qué ves?
—Levántate.
—Tira de la cuerda o toca el timbre.
—Camina a la puerta de salida.
—Agárrate a la barra.
—Baja.
—Espera otro autobús.
—Sube.
—Busca un asiento libre, camina al asiento y siéntate.

Quiz 4 (Classes 33 - 42)

See section on Tests at the end of the book.

Final Exam (Skit)

See section on Tests at the end of the book.

Tests

Quiz 1 .... Classes   1 - 5
Quiz 2 .... Classes   6 - 13
Midterm. .... Classes   1 - 19
Quiz 3 .... Classes 20 - 32
Quiz 4 .... Classes 33 - 42
Final Skit

For directions on how to administer the tests, see the section on Testing in the Introduction. Capital letters in parentheses are used to identify several versions of the same quiz or test. The numbers in parentheses after each command indicate the number of points assigned to each command or question. Blanks stand for actual students' names taking the quizzes at the time, to be filled by you as you give the commands orally. Read the whole command clearly at normal speed, and wait for the student to act. Do not repeat commands more than twice. If the student makes an error, write what he/she did, on the paper, for later reference. As mentioned in the Introduction, do not allow the students to see the quiz before or after the exam until it has been graded. On grading these quizzes, we suggest that you give credit for a command performed half or partially right. For example, if when given a two-point command such as *Corre a la pizarra*, the student runs to the table instead, you credit him/her with one point for *corre*. Therefore, tell the class before quiz day that if they understand a command only partially, they should perform what they know so they can get some credit. For instance, if the student understands *corre* in the command "Corre a la pizarra," the student should run somewhere even if he/she does not understand "pizarra" in order to get points for running.

Should you decide to use these quizzes, you will need to study them ahead of time to see which props you need to administer them. When setting up for these testing sessions, it is always a good idea to display "distractors" in the classroom, that is, more items than just those absolutely required to perform the command correctly, so that the student has to make a selection among several familiar items. For instance if the commands read "*Toca el libro rojo*," you need to have three or four books of different colors on the table.

The commands that follow are recombinations of items that students know but perhaps have never encountered in this particular sequence. If students are able to understand a sentence they have never heard before, that shows they are in their way to fluency.

QUIZ 1 (Classes 1 - 5)
Quiz 1 (A)

28 puntos   Nombre _____

1. Escriba su dirección en un papel blanco. (4)
2. Abra la boca y cierre la boca. (3)
3. Siéntese en la mesa y ríase. (3)
4. Camine a la ventana, dé la vuelta y señale la puerta. (5)
5. Camine a la silla, siéntese y tóquese las rodillas. (5)
6. Abra / cierre las dos puertas. (3)
7. Toque la pared con las dos manos. (5)

Quiz 1 (B)

34 puntos Nombre _____

1. Camine a la pizarra. Dibuje un círculo y un cuadrado alrededor del círculo. (7)
2. Siéntese debajo de la mesa y grite. (4)
3. Coja la revista y el lápiz. Deje el lápiz junto a la ventana. (6)
4. Toque a _____ en la nariz y ríase. (4)
5. Coja un papel y una pluma de la mesa. Escriba el número _____ en el papel. (8)
6. Cierre los ojos y abra los ojos. (3)
7. Señale el reloj. (2)

Quiz 1 (C)

39 puntos Nombre _____

1. Coja el libro rojo y póngalo en el suelo. (5)
2. Ponga la flor entre la pluma amarilla y la pluma azul. (6)
3. Encienda / apague la luz, coja el número 9 de la pizarra y déselo a _____. (8)
4. Tírele de la oreja a _____ y golpéele en el hombro. (5)
5. Corte un papel amarillo y póngalo debajo de la puerta. (6)
6. Siéntese en la silla y ponga los pies en la mesa. (5)
7. Ponga una tiza en el libro. (4)

Quiz 1 (D)

33 puntos Nombre _____

1. Camine a la pizarra, escriba su nombre y señale la silla. (6)
2. Toque la ventana y deme el libro. (4)
3. Ponga el papel amarillo en el suelo. (4)
4. Escriba el número once en la pizarra. (4)
5. Dibuje un reloj en el papel blanco. (4)
6. Dele el gato a _____. (3)
7. Dame la mano. (3)
8. Salta a la pared. (2)
9. Tírale la tiza a _____. (3)

Quiz 1 (E)

30 puntos   Nombre _____

1. Señala el techo con la pluma azul. (4)
2. Apaga / Enciende la luz y siéntate. (3)
3. Camina alrededor de la sala de clase (3)
4. Camine, párese, dé la vuelta y salte. (4)
5. Toca el papel rosa de la mesa y tócate la cara. (6)
6. Dale la flor a _____ . (3)
7. Corte un papel azul y un papel blanco, y póngalos debajo de la silla. (7)

QUIZ 2 (Classes 6 - 13)

Note to the Reading Sections:

Have one copy of each Reading Section printed in large letters. Hand this copy to the student only by the time he/she gets to the Reading Section of the quiz. Prompt the student ("Haz el número 1," "Haz el número 2," etc.), and, as the student performs the actions, do the grading on your copy of the quiz.

Quiz 2 (A)

39 puntos   Nombre _____

1. Coge el pantalón corto y la chaqueta. (5)
2. Deja caer la cuchara y el cuchillo en el suelo. (4)
3. Pon la camisa en la percha. (3)
4. Corre alrededor de la mesa; baila y canta. (5)
5. Sécate las manos con la toalla y péinate. (4)

Reading Section

1. Señala la leche. (2)
2. Busca una corbata y unos calcetines. (3)
3. Sostén el jabón en la mano derecha y la naranja en la mano izquierda. (6)
4. Duerme, ronca y despierta. (3)
5. Echa café en la taza y bebe. (4)

Quiz 2 (B)

44 puntos   Nombre _____

1. Cepíllate los dientes y quítate los zapatos. (4)
2. Cuenta las luces de la clase. (4)
3. Ponte el sombrero, coge el paraguas y mira la ventana. (6)
4. Tírale la pelota a _____. (3)
5. Coge el vestido del departamento de señoras. (4)

Reading Section

1. Pon la camisa, la corbata y la chaqueta en una percha. (5)
2. Ponte triste, enfádate y llora. (4)
3. Echa un poco de café en la taza. (4)
4. Cuenta los dólares que están en la mesa. (6)
5. (Des)abrocha dos botones de la camisa. (4)

Quiz 2 (C)

44 puntos Nombre _____
1. Levanta el vaso y bota la pelota cinco veces. (6)
2. Mira a _____ y abrázalo (-la). (3)
3. Busca la falda y el suéter. (3)
4. Rápidamente quítate los zapatos y camina lentamente a la puerta. (7)
5. Ponte la chaqueta azul. (3)

Reading Section
1. Lávate las manos con el jabón y sécate con la toalla. (5)
2. Ponte el suéter y quítatelo. (3)
3. Tírale la manzana a _____. (3)
4. Duerme en el suelo; ronca y despierta; levántate y cepíllate los dientes. (7)
5. Ponte el sombrero y abre el paraguas. (4)

Quiz 2 (D)

36 puntos Nombre _____
1. Echa jugo de naranja en la taza. (4)
2. Péinate con el peine rojo. (3)
3. Cuenta las cucharas. (2)
4. Quítate el zapato derecho. (3)
5. Saca la pasta de dientes. (3)
6. Compra los pantalones de color gris. (3)

Reading Section
1. Muestra la pera y la banana. (3)
2. Lávate las manos con el jabón. (4)
3. Cepíllate los dientes. (2)
4. Ponte el abrigo. (2)
5. Bebe agua y grita. (3)
6. Ponte la chaqueta y quítatela (4)

MIDTERM EXAM
(Classes 1 -19) (Exhibits 1 - 4)

In some cases, besides understanding the commands and performing the appropriate actions, the student is expected to speak by providing short answers to questions. The Reading Section provided here for the midterm is identical for all versions of the exam (A, B, C and D), but you can certainly write your own for each one. To make it faster, the whole class can also take the Reading Section at the same time by providing a copy to students, and they will simply write an English translation of the commands, if English is their first language. For the third question of the Reading Section you will need to show a picture of a woman performing an action, and your students will need to write down in Spanish what she is doing.

Midterm Exam (A)

79 puntos   Nombre _____

1. Habla español. (3)
2. Coge la foto del hombre que está nervioso. Siéntate y golpea el suelo con el pie muchas veces. (10)
3. Lee el periódico. (2)
4. Siéntate delante de _____. (3)
5. Muéstrame el tenedor y el cuchillo. (3)
6. Señala el día de hoy en el calendario. (Pause.) ¿Es hoy martes? (5)
7. (Show a picture and ask:) ¿Qué hace este hombre? (4)
8. Ponte el impermeable amarillo. (3)
9. Ponte el vaso vacío en la cabeza (4)
10. (Show the student a dirty piece of paper and ask:) ¿Está el papel limpio o sucio? (4)

Reading Section (for all)

11. Deja caer la pluma en tu bolso (4)
12. Pon una pera sobre los pantalones. (3)
13. (Show a picture and ask:) ¿Qué hace la mujer? (3)
14. Camina a la mesa y coge una tiza. (4)
15. Abre el calendario en el mes de noviembre. (Pause.) ¿Es noviembre el último mes del año? (7)
16. Señala a un estudiante que lleva unos pantalones azules claros. (6)
17. Señala las fotos de la mujer guapa y el hombre feo. (6)
18. Salta, grita, golpea la mesa y corre. (5)

Midterm Exam (B)

79 puntos   Nombre _____

1. Camina a la pared y apaga la luz. (4)
2. Ponte el lápiz en la oreja. (3)
3. Ve a la mesa y coge una taza. (4)
4. Levanta la mano derecha. (Pause.) ¿Puedes tocar el techo? (4)
5. Dale dinero a _____. (3)
6. Señala la foto de la mujer guapa y el hombre feo. (5)
7. (Show a picture and ask:) ¿Qué hace este niño? (4)
8. Pon una pera sobre los pantalones. (4)
9. Abre el calendario en el mes de noviembre. (Pause.) ¿Estamos hoy a cuatro de noviembre? (6)
10. Ponte la camisa azul oscura. (4)

Reading Section (for all)

11. Deja caer la pluma en tu bolso (4)
12. Pon una pera sobre los pantalones. (3)
13. (Show a picture and ask:) ¿Qué hace la mujer? (3)

14. Camina a la mesa y coge una tiza. (4)
15. Abre el calendario en el mes de noviembre. (Pause.) ¿Es noviembre el último mes del año? (7)
16. Señala a un estudiante que lleva unos pantalones azules claros. (6)
17. Señala las fotos de la mujer guapa y el hombre feo. (6)
18. Salta, grita, golpea la mesa y corre. (5)

Midterm Exam (C)

79 puntos   *Nombre* _____

1. Dale la mano a _____. Tócale el hombro con la mano izquierda. (6)
2. Mira por la ventana y coge el paraguas. (4)
3. Echale un poco de agua en la mano a _____. (Pause.) ¿Está la mano mojada o seca? (6)
4. Señala el día de la semana en el calendario. (Pause.) ¿Es hoy viernes? (5)
5. Señala la foto del hombre que está asustado. (4)
6. ¿Qué hace la mujer? (4)
7. Señala tus zapatos. ¿De qué color son? (4)
8. ¿Cuántos años tiene él? (2)
9. Salta diez veces rápidamente. ¿Estás cansado? (6)

Reading Section (for all)

10. Deja caer la pluma en tu bolso (4)
11. Pon una pera sobre los pantalones. (3)
12. (Show a picture and ask:) ¿Qué hace la mujer? (3)
13. Camina a la mesa y coge una tiza. (4)
14. Abre el calendario en el mes de noviembre. (Pause.) ¿Es noviembre el último mes del año? (7)
15. Señala a un estudiante que lleva unos pantalones azules claros. (6)
16. Señala las fotos de la mujer guapa y el hombre feo. (6)
17. Salta, grita, golpea la mesa y corre. (5)

Midterm Exam (D)

79 puntos   *Nombre* _____

1. Baila con _____. (3)
2. Siéntate junto a la ventana. Mira por la ventana y dibuja un paraguas en la pizarra. (7)
3. Echa un poco de agua en la mano de _____. (Pause.) ¿Está la mano mojada o seca? (6)
4. Señala el día de la semana en el calendario. (Pause.) ¿Es hoy sábado? (5)
5. Actúa como si estuvieras cansado. Siéntate en la mesa. (5)
6. (Show a picture and ask:) ¿Qué hacen estos hombres? (4)
7. (Show a picture of a child's birthday party, and ask:) ¿Cuántos años tiene? (4)

8. Mueve el jugo de naranja. (3)

9. Ponte el vestido amarillo y negro (4)

Reading Section (for all)

10. Deja caer la pluma en tu bolso (4)

11. Pon una pera sobre los pantalones. (3)

12. ¿Qué hace la mujer? (3)

13. Camina a la mesa y coge una tiza. (4)

14. Abre el calendario en el mes de noviembre. (Pause.) ¿Es noviembre el último mes del año? (7)

15. Señala a un estudiante que lleva unos pantalones azules claros. (6)

16. Señala las fotos de la mujer guapa y el hombre feo. (6)

17. Salta, grita, golpea la mesa y corre. (5)

Quiz 3 (Classes 20 - 32)

190 puntos, including the Reading Section printed on the Student Answer Sheet for Quiz 3.

This quiz can be administered to the entire class a the same time. First you will find the script for you to read from. Then there is a Student Answer Sheet that you can reproduce for students to write on.

I. Datos personales (10 puntos)
<u>LISTEN AND WRITE DOWN THE INFORMATION REQUESTED</u>

1. Escriba su nombre y su apellido. (2)

2. Escriba su dirección: calle, número, ciudad, estado y districto postal. (6)

3. Escriba su edad (¿Cuántos años tiene? (1)

4. Escriba su profesión. (1)

II. La hora (21 puntos)
<u>LISTEN AND DRAW CLOCKS OR WRITE DOWN TIMES USING NUMBERS</u>

1. Dibujen un reloj a las seis menos veinte. (3)

2. Son las seis en punto. (3)

3. Pongan el reloj a las siete y media. (3)

4. Son las nueve y trece minutos. (3)

5. Pongan el reloj a las cuatro menos cuarto. (3)

6. Son las dos menos cinco. (3)

7. Dibujen un reloj a las ocho y cuarto. (3)

III. Las profesiones y la ciudad (63 puntos)
<u>LISTEN AND WRITE DOWN AN ENGLISH TRANSLATION</u>

1. Vaya a la gasolinera y eche gasolina. (4)

2. Los niños estuvieron en la escuela. (3)

3. Los sábado voy al parque. Los domingos voy a la iglesia. (6)

4. Los lunes voy a la biblioteca. (3)

5. En octubre voy al teatro. (3)
6. El hombre se cortó el pelo en la barbería. (4)
7. Compré ropa en los grandes almacenes. (3)
8. Camina a la farmacia. Camina a Correos a echar una carta. (6)
9. Esta es mi casa. (3)
10. Las mujeres están en el supermercado. (3)
11. Fue a la panadería y compró pan. (4)
12. El estuvo en el hospital. (3)
13. ¿Qué es esto? (3)
14. ¿Es este hombre abogado? (3)
15. ¿Es esta mujer secretaria? (3)
16. ¿Está la panadería junto al banco? (4)
17. ¿Está la iglesia entre el cine y el restaurante? (5)

IV. El supermercado y el restaurante (48 puntos)
LISTEN AND WRITE DOWN AN ENGLISH TRANSLATION

1. Toca las fresas y las peras. (3)
2. Los tomates están junto a los limones. (4)
3. Compra leche y huevos. (3)
4. Dame la mantequilla. (2)
5. Pusieron una botella de vino en la casta. (4)
6. Pon la lechuga con las verduras. (3)
7. Pon el queso entre la carne y el pescado. (5)
8. Trae un vaso de agua para los clientes. (4)
9. Pon la mesa. (2)
10. Pollo frito con patatas fritas y verduras para la señora. (5)
11. ¿Me da una servilleta y un cuchillo, por favor? (4)
12. El señor pidió un plato de sopa. (4)
13. Por favor, una taza de café. (3)
14. ¿Cómo estás? (2)
    Bien gracias.

Quiz 3 (Classes 20 - 32)
Student Answer Sheet

190 puntos   *Nombre* _____

I. Datos personales (10 puntos)
LISTEN AND WRITE DOWN THE INFORMATION REQUESTED

1. _____
2. _____
3. _____
4. _____

II. La hora (21 points)
LISTEN AND DRAW CLOCKS OR WRITE DOWN TIMES USING NUMBERS

1. _____
2. _____
3. _____
4. _____
5. _____
6. _____
7. _____

III. Las profesiones y la ciudad (63 puntos)
LISTEN AND WRITE DOWN AN ENGLISH TRANSLATION

1. _____
2. _____
3. _____
4. _____
5. _____
6. _____
7. _____
8. _____
9. _____

10. _____
11. _____
12. _____
13. _____
14. _____
15. _____
16. _____
17. _____

IV. El supermercado y el restaurante (48 puntos)
LISTEN AND WRITE DOWN AN ENGLISH TRANSLATION

1. _____
2. _____
3. _____
4. _____
5. _____
6. _____
7. _____
8. _____
9. _____
10. _____
11. _____
12. _____
13. _____
14. _____

V. Reading Section (48 puntos)

WRITE DOWN AN ENGLISH TRANSLATION FOR THE FOLLOWING SENTENCES

1. Dibuje un reloj a las tres menos cuarto. (4)
2. Es domingo. Ve a la iglesia. (3)
3. Usted es arquitecto. Muestre los dibujos de una casa. (5)
4. Tú eres mecánico. Ponte debajo del coche. (5)
5. Ve a la farmacia. (2)
6. Pon al hombre delante de las frutas y verduras. (5)
7. Pon a la mujer que empuja el carro de la compra delante de la caja registradora. (7)
8. Coma una hamburguesa con patatas fritas. (3)
9. Pon la comida en la cesta. (3)
10. ¿Corta carne el carnicero? (3)
11. ¿Cuánto cuestan las fresas? (3)
12. Pon los grandes almacenes entre la panadería y la escuela. (5)

Quiz 4 (Classes 33- 42)

364 puntos *Nombre* _____

This quiz can be administered to the entire class a the same time. First you will find the script for you to read from. Then there is a Student Answer Sheet that you can reproduce for students to write on.

I. Geografía y Viajes (83 puntos)

TRANSLATE INTO ENGLISH

1. Hay un valle grande entre las montañas. (4)
2. El río es muy ancho cuando llega al mar. (6)
3. Los turistas van en autobús. (3)
4. Hay barcos en el río. (3)
5. Podemos ver personas que caminan en la calle. (5)
6. La torre es muy alta. (3)
7. Hay mucho tráfico. (3)
8. La familia viaja en coche (carro). (3)
9. Hay tres países en Norteamérica. (4)
10. Florida es una península. (3)
11. Cuba es una isla. (3)
12. Las Montañas Rocosas están en Norteamérica. (4)
13. El Océano Pacífico está al oeste de los Estados Unidos. (5)
14. El Mississippi es un río. (3)
15. México está al sur de los Estados Unidos. (4)
16. Inglaterra es una isla cerca de la costa de Francia. (6)
17. Madrid es la capital de España. (4)
18. En Brasil se habla portugués. (3)

ANSWER THE QUESTIONS IN SPANISH

19. ¿De dónde es usted? (4)
20. ¿Viviste en Costa Rica? (3)

DRAW WHAT IT SAYS

21. Dibuje el mapa de Norteamérica. (3)
22. Señala en el mapa de dónde son tus padres. (4)

II. El futuro (14 puntos)
TRANSLATE INTO ENGLISH

23. Él va a hacer la cama. (3)

ANSWER THE QUESTIONS IN SPANISH

24. ¿Qué vas a hacer el sábado? (6)
25. ¿Qué ropa vas a llevar (ponerte) mañana? (6)

III. La familia (20 puntos)
TRANSLATE INTO ENGLISH

26. Estos son mis padres. (3)
27. Tengo dos sobrinos. (3)
28. La tercera, a la derecha, es mi hermana. (4)

ANSWER THE QUESTION IN SPANISH

29. ¿Cómo se llama tu hermano? (5)

DRAW WHAT IT SAYS

30. Dibuje el árbol genealógico de su familia. (5)

IV. La casa (131 puntos)
TRANSLATE INTO ENGLISH

31. Esta es mi casa. (4)
32. Los niños están en la cama de los padres. (4)
33. Hay platos y tazas en el armario. (4)
34. El sofá y los sillones están en la sala de estar. (4)
35. Hay tres cuadros en la pared de la sala de estar. (5)
36. Hay un puchero rojo en la cocina de gas. (4)
37. La madre duerme en el suelo de la cocina. (4)
38. Hay una lámpara sobre la cómoda roja. (5)
39. No hay un gato en el dormitorio de los niños. (4)
40. Hay un espejo en el cuarto de baño. (3)
41. Pon la mesa para dos personas. (4)
42. Barre el suelo con la escoba. (3)
43. Pon al hombre en la cocina. (3)
44. Pon el sofá marrón en la sala de estar. (4)

45. Pon una toalla blanca y el espejo pequeño en el cuarto de baño. (6)
46. Pon la cama grande en el dormitorio de la izquierda. (5)
47. Pon la estantería de libros en la sala de estar. (3)
48. Señala el fregadero y la lavadora. (3)
49. Pon la cafetera en la mesa. (3)
50. Pon dos tazas sucias en el lavaplatos. (5)
51. Pon las verduras en el frigorífico. (3)
52. Pon el perro y el gato debajo de la mesa. (5)
53. Pon las cortinas rojas y blancas en la ventana del cuarto de baño. (6)
54. Pon la maceta de flores en el jardín. (4)
55. Pon la mesita de noche en el dormitorio de la niña. (5)
56. Pon la lámpara en el techo. (3)
57. Pon el váter (inodoro) en el cuarto de baño. (3)
58. Pon la mesita de centro en la sala de estar. (4)
59. Pon el cubo delante de la lavadora. (4)
60. Contesta el teléfono. (2)
61. Saca la ropa de la secadora. (4)
62. Hay una silla entre el hombre y el niño. (5)
63. Pon un pollo en el horno. (3)

V. Descripción de objetos / personas; contrastes (78 puntos)
TRANSLATE INTO ENGLISH

64. Es un hombre alto. (3)
65. Es una naranja; es pequeña; es una fruta. (4)
66. Es un rectángulo; es rojo, azul y blanco. (4)
67. ¿Qué es esto? (4)

ANSWER THE QUESTION IN SPANISH

You need to show the students a picture of a man.
68. ¿Cómo es este hombre? (6)

TRANSLATE INTO ENGLISH

69. Los niños son bajos. (3)
70. Es un niño gordo. (3)
71. El hombre es muy fuerte. (3)
72. La mujer es joven y tiene el pelo corto. (5)
73. El agua está fría. (3)
74. La casa es pequeña. (3)
75. Esta mujer es vieja. (3)
76. Pancho Carrancho es gordo y feo. (4)
77. El estudiante es muy inteligente. (3)
78. La muchacha es muy delgada. (3)
79. Este hombre tiene el pelo blanco y es muy viejo. (5)

80. No puedo levantar el coche porque es demasiado pesado. (6)
81. La aspiradora es nueva. (3)
82. ¿Son estos hombres viejos o jóvenes? (4)

ANSWER QUESTION IN SPANISH

83. ¿Cómo es usted? (6)

VI. El coche (auto) (38 puntos)

TRANSLATE INTO ENGLISH

84. Abróchese el cinturón de seguridad. (3)
85. Ponga la llave. (2)
86. Quite el freno de mano. (3)
87. Ponga el pie izquierdo en el embrague y el pie derecho en el acelerador. (7)
88. Ponga la mano en el cambio de marchas y meta la primera. (5)
89. Conduzca el coche. (2)
90. Ponga la radio. (2)
91. Eche el intermitente y vuelva a la izquierda. (4)
92. Todo recto. Todo seguido. (2)
93. Eche el intermitente y vuelva a la derecha. (4)
94. Ponga el pie en el freno y pare. (4)

Quiz 4 (Classes 33 - 42)
Student Answer Sheet

364 puntos   *Nombre* _____

I. Geografía y Viajes (83 puntos)

TRANSLATE INTO ENGLISH

1. _____
2. _____
3. _____
4. _____
5. _____
6. _____
7. _____
8. _____
9. _____
10. _____

11. _____
12. _____
13. _____
14. _____
15. _____
16. _____
17. _____
18. _____

ANSWER THE QUESTIONS IN SPANISH

19. _____
20. _____

DRAW WHAT IS SAYS

21. _____
22. _____

II. El futuro (14 puntos)
TRANSLATE INTO ENGLISH

23. _____

ANSWER THE QUESTIONS IN SPANISH

24. _____
25. _____

III. La familia (20 puntos)
TRANSLATE INTO ENGLISH

26. _____
27. _____
28. _____

ANSWER THE QUESTION IN SPANISH

29. _____

DRAW WHAT IT SAYS

30. _____

IV. La casa (131 puntos)
TRANSLATE INTO ENGLISH

31. _____
32. _____
33. _____
34. _____
35. _____
36. _____
37. _____
38. _____
39. _____
40. _____
41. _____
42. _____
43. _____
44. _____
45. _____
46. _____
47. _____
48. _____
49. _____
50. _____
51. _____
52. _____
53. _____
54. _____
55. _____

56. _____
57. _____
58. _____
59. _____
60. _____
61. _____
62. _____
63. _____

V. Descripción de objetos / personas; contrastes (78 puntos)
TRANSLATE INTO ENGLISH

64. _____
65. _____
66. _____
67. _____

ANSWER THE QUESTION IN SPANISH

68. _____

TRANSLATE INTO ENGLISH

69. _____
70. _____
71. _____
72. _____
73. _____
74. _____
75. _____
76. _____
77. _____
78. _____
79. _____

80. _____

81. _____

82. _____

ANSWER QUESTION IN SPANISH

83. _____

VI. El coche (auto) (38 puntos)
TRANSLATE INTO ENGLISH

84. _____

85. _____

86. _____

87. _____

88. _____

89. _____

90. _____

91. _____

92. _____

93. _____

94. _____

FINAL EXAM: Skits

Divide the class into groups of three or four students. Each will prepare a skit in Spanish to be presented to the entire class. What follows are some guidelines on how to go about it.

1. When you organize the groups make sure the overall level of ability is similar.
2. Ask the students to think first of a dramatic situation. By this we mean a situation in which there is much action. Before students start writing down a script they should have a clear idea of what they are going to do, that is, what is going to happen, what story they are going to tell through physical actions and movement. They should ask themselves before they start writing, the following questions: Where are we? Who is there? What is happening? Why? How does the story begin? How does it end? By emphasizing this, you avoid the problem of having students try verbal exchanges for which they do not have the vocabulary or grammatical structures. It's always easier to prepare a situation like those experienced in class (supermarket, clothing store, gas station, etc.) However, students always come up with the most original variations on these, and other very original ones. At any rate, they should stick to the vocabulary they have internalized in class, and stay away from the dictionary in search of unfamiliar vocabulary.
3. Once they have a visual idea of how they are going to stage the skit, they should block it on the stage, and mime the actions without saying anything, as in a dumb show or silent film.
4. The next step will be to add words here and there, to add a sound track, so to speak.
5. Finally, students can write a second version with a fuller text.
6. Students should rehearse at least once before performing the skit. This rehearsal could be videotaped. By doing this, they have a chance to see whether or not it's going to work. You can also make suggestions in terms of the staging, and help them fine tune the grammar and vocabulary.
7. Tell them that no notes or scripts will be allowed during the performance.
8. Emphasize to them that their work will not be graded on the written skit they have produced, but on the performed skit itself, that is on the communicative effectiveness of their performance, attending to both language and action.
9. You will need to decide whether their work will be a graded as a group product, or each student will be graded individually.
10. Videotape their skits. Although some students may object, they'll love to see them later. An alternative is to have students videotape their skits at home, and then simply play the video during the final.
11. Allow two classes for groups to create and rehearse their skits. You should make all props used during the course available to students should they need some for their skits.
12. You could give them the option of videotaping their skits outside of class, and then playing their videos in class instead of performing live in front of the class.

Here are the suggested criteria and point allotment to grade the skits.

Vocabulary	(20%)	____%
Intonation	(20%)	____%
Pronunciation	(20%)	____%
Delivery and Proyection	(20%)	____%
Space and Movement	(15%)	____%
Props and Costumes	(5%)	____%
	Total	100 points

Please note: Students cannot use notes or scripts during the performance.

Skits Grading Sheet
PROYECTO FINAL DE PRODUCCION ORAL EN GRUPOS

(100 puntos)

Grupo _____   Nombre (s) _____   Puntos _____

      Vocabulario .... (20)   _____

      Entonación .... (20)   _____

      Pronunciación .... (20)   _____

      Proyección .... (20)   _____

      Espacio y movimiento .... (15)   _____

      Utilería y vestuario .... (5)   _____

                                     Total   _____

TPR PRODUCTS

**Books • Games
Student Kits
Teacher Kits
Audio Cassettes
Video Demonstrations**

Order directly from the publisher using your
<u>*VISA*</u>*,* <u>*MASTERCARD*</u>*, or* <u>*DISCOVER CARD*</u>
WE SHIP ASAP TO ANYWHERE IN THE WORLD!

Sky Oaks Productions, Inc.
Since 1973
P.O. Box 1102
Los Gatos, CA 95031 USA

Phone: (408) 395-7600
Fax: (408) 395-8440
E-mail: tprworld@aol.com

FREE CATALOG UPON REQUEST!

 For fast service,
order online by clicking on:

www.tpr-world.com

Introduction
by the Originator of TPR, Dr. James J. Asher

Dear Colleague,

If you are new to TPR, start with a solid understanding by reading my book, **Learning Another Language Through Actions** (6th edition) and Ramiro Garcia's **Instructor's Notebook: How to apply TPR for best results** (4th edition).

To insure success, pretest a few lessons before you enter your classroom. Try the lessons out with your children, your friends or your neighbors. In doing this, you

(a) become convinced that TPR actually works,

(b) build self-confidence in the approach, and

(c) smooth out your delivery.

For Students of All Ages, including Adults

Use TPR for new vocabulary and grammar, to help your students immediately understand the target language in chunks rather than word-by-word. This instant success is absolutely thrilling for students. You will hear them say to each other, "Wow! I actually understand what the instructor is saying."

After a "silent period" of about three weeks listening to you and following your directions in the target language (without translation), your students will be ready to talk, read and write. In our books, Ramiro and I will guide you step-by-step along the way.

This catalog is loaded with activities that will keep your students excited day after day as they move towards fluency in the target language

Best wishes for continued success,

James J Asher

Latest books by James J. Asher

Brainswitching:
Learning on the Right Side of the Brain

2nd Ed. - 308 Pages   For *Fast*, *Stress-Free* *Access* to   Order #202
Languages, Mathematics, Science, and much, much more!

The Super School:
Teaching on the Right Side of the Brain
*To help most students learn anything fast
in academics, sports, or technology!*
Your students won't want to miss a single class!   Order #204

New! The Weird and Wonderful World of
Mathematical Mysteries
Conversations with famous scientists and mathematicians.
by James J. Asher   Order #91a

Exclusive - New discovery published here for the first time solves a 2,000 year old mystery that baffled such famous people as Pythagoras, Euclid, Sir Isaac Newton, and Einstein.

- With TPR, I demonstrate how to remove the fear of learning foreign languages. With this new book, I show you how to remove the fear of mathematics.
- My conversations with famous scientists and mathematicians reveals their secret strategy for making spectacular breakthroughs by playing with ideas on the right side of the brain.
- I demonstrate how anyone who can do simple arithmetic has a shot at world fame by finding hidden patterns in nature!

A Simplified Guide to Statistics for Non-Mathematicians:
How to organize a successful research project.
by James J. Asher   Order #265

New!
- How to evaluate the effectiveness of your instructional program to get the support you deserve from your organization.
- Here is my promise: If you can do simple arithmetic, you will understand *every concept* in this easy-to-read book!
- Learn the ABC's of any first-class research program.

Added Bonus: Tips for organizing a successful master's thesis or doctoral dissertation!

The Latest from James J. Asher

Originator of the Total Physical Response, known worldwide as TPR

✓ **Demonstrates** step-by-step **how to apply TPR** to help children and adults acquire another language **without stress.**

✓ More than **150 hours** of **classroom-tested TPR lessons** that **can be adapted to teach any language** including Arabic, Chinese, English, French, German, Hebrew, Spanish, Japanese, and Russian.

Order #201

✓ A behind-the-scenes look at how **TPR** was developed.
✓ **Answers over 100 frequently asked questions** about **TPR.**
✓ **Easy to understand** summary of 25 years of research with Dr. Asher's world famous **Total Physical Response.**

NEW FEATURES
• Frequently Asked Questions - Newly Expanded! • Letters from my mailbag
• e-mail addresses for TPR instructors around the world

New! *James J. Asher's* Prize-Winning TPR Research

Order #7-CD

For the first time collected in one place on a CD, the complete prize-winning body of research by James J. Asher. Booklet available with the CD gives Asher's comments on each study with recommendations for future research. Saves you weeks of searching the internet or library.
• Shows step-by-step how Asher planned and successfully completed each research study.
• Includes all of Asher's pioneer studies in second language learning.

Bonus: Also includes Asher's research in industrial psychology—problem solving, creativity, hiring, training, aptitude testing, and designing the world's first automated postal distribution center.

New! *James J. Asher's* Brainstorming Kit

Transforms <u>ordinary</u> <u>committee</u> <u>meetings</u> into high-powered problem solving sessions!

Order #8

• Booklet and Transparencies with step-by-step directions to guide your brainstorming group.
• Helps your group understand what to do and why they are doing it.
• Discover options you never thought possible—and it's a lot of fun, too!

Dear Colleague:

Language instructors often say to me, "I tried the TPR lessons in your book and my students responded with great enthusiasm, but what can the students do **at their seats**?"

Here are effective TPR activities that students can perform **at their seats**. Each student has a kit such as the interior of a kitchen. Then you say in the target language, "Put the man in front of the sink." With your kit displayed so that it is clearly visible to the students, you place the man in the kitchen of your kit and your students follow by performing the same action in their kits.

As items are internalized, you can gradually discontinue the modeling. Eventually, you will utter a direction and the students will quickly respond without being shown what to do.

Each figure in the **TPR Student Kits** will stick to any location on the playboard **without glue**. Just press and the figure is on. It can be peeled off instantly and placed in a different location over and over.

You can create fresh sentences that give students practice in understanding hundreds of useful vocabulary items and grammatical structures. Also, students quickly acquire "function" words such as **up, down, on, off, under, over, next to, in front of,** and **behind**.

To guide you step-by-step I have written ten complete lessons for each kit (giving you about 200 commands for each kit design), and those lessons are now available in your choice of **English, Spanish, French,** or **German**. The kits can be used with **children or adults** who are learning **any language** including **ESL** and the **sign language of the deaf**.

About the TPR Teacher Kits

Use the **transparencies** with an overhead projector to flash a playboard on a large screen. Your students **listen** to you utter a direction in the target language, **watch** you perform the action on the large screen, and then follow by performing the same action in their **Student Kits**.

Best wishes for continued success,

James J. Asher

P.S.
My sister and I recently tried one of the Student Kits with a native speaker of Arabic giving directions. We were both surprised at how much vocabulary and grammar we picked up in only a few minutes of play.

Total Physical Fun
by Jo Ann Olliphant

For language teachers at all levels who wish to enhance learning through the power of play!

$29.00
Order No. 94

- 100 Games field-tested with all ages from preschoolers to adults
- Students learn more easily when they are involved in interesting and entertaining activities
- For students at all levels learning any new language
- No special preparation necessary

Jo Ann Olliphant

Frees the instructor from routine, rote, and mindless repetition.

Back By Popular Demand!

For every 5 Kits (Student or Teacher) in <u>any</u> assortment, select an additional kit as our **Free Gift** to you!

James J. Asher's TPR STUDENT KITS™

More than 300,000 Kits now being used in FL-ESL classes throughout the world!!

	ENGLISH Order Number	SPANISH Order Number	FRENCH Order Number	GERMAN Order Number	DUTCH Order Number
Airport ©	4E	4S	4F	4G	4D
Beach ©	12E	12S	12F	12G	12D
Classroom ©	10E	10S	10F	10G	10D
Garden ©	17E	17S	17F	17G	17D
Department Store ©	13E	13S	13F	13G	13D
Farm ©	60E	60S	60F	60G	60D
Gas Station ©	5E	5S	5F	5G	5D
Home ©	1E	1S	1F	1G	1D
Hospital ©	21E	21S	21F	21G	21D
Kitchen ©	2E	2S	2F	2G	2D
Main Street ©	15E	15S	15F	15G	15D
New ➤ Office ©	6E	6S	6F	6G	n/a

(Includes high tech business machines such as computers, cell phones, and even satellite communications!)

	ENGLISH	SPANISH	FRENCH	GERMAN	DUTCH
Picnic ©	16E	16S	16F	16G	16D
Playground ©	20E	20S	20F	20G	20D
Restaurant ©	40E	40S	40F	40G	40D
Supermarket ©	11E	11S	11F	11G	11D
Town ©	3E	3S	3F	3G	3D
United States Map ©	22E	22S	22F	n/a	22D
New ➤ European Map ©	23E	23S	23F	23G	23D

(Recently updated to include the Middle East!)

4-KITS-IN-ONE: Community, School, Work, Leisure © 50E 50S 50F 50G 50D
Calendar © (limited supply) .... 31 (In English)
TPR Student Kit Stories © Uses vocabulary from the **Student Kits**.   Order Number 33

TPR TEACHER KITS™
Transparencies for an <u>Overhead</u> Projector

	ENGLISH Order Number	SPANISH Order Number	FRENCH Order Number	GERMAN Order Number	DUTCH Order Number
Airport ©	4ET	4ST	4FT	4GT	4DT
Beach ©	12ET	12ST	12FT	12GT	12DT
Classroom ©	10ET	10ST	10FT	10GT	10DT
Garden ©	17ET	17ST	17FT	17GT	17DT
Dept. Store ©	13ET	13ST	13FT	13GT	13DT
Farm ©	60ET	60ST	60FT	60GT	60DT
Home ©	1ET	1ST	1FT	1GT	1DT
Hospital ©	21ET	21ST	21FT	21GT	21DT
Kitchen ©	2ET	2ST	2FT	2GT	2DT
Main Street ©	15ET	15ST	15FT	15GT	15DT
New ➤ Office ©	6ET	6ST	6FT	6GT	n/a
Picnic ©	16ET	16ST	16FT	16GT	16DT
Playground ©	20ET	20ST	20FT	20GT	20DT
Supermarket ©	11ET	11ST	11FT	11GT	11DT
Town ©	3ET	3ST	3FT	3GT	3DT
U.S. Map ©	22ET	22ST	22FT	22GT	22DT
New ➤ European Map ©	23ET	23ST	23FT	23GT	23DT

See all of the **TPR Student Kits** in <u>Full Color</u>:
click on: www.tpr-world.com
look in: "Learning Another Language Through Actions"
look in: "Instructor's Notebook: How to apply TPR for best results!"

Best Demonstrations of Classic TPR *Anywhere in the World!*

James J. Asher's Classic Videos demonstrate the original research...

Historic videos show the original TPR research by Dr. James J. Asher with children and adults learning Japanese, Spanish, French and German. These vintage demonstrations are time-tested, and even more valid today than when the film was shot decades ago. We include with every video a copy of the scientific publications documenting the amazing results you will see. A must for anyone teaching TPR. Each video is unique, and shows different stress-free features of TPR instruction — *no matter what language you are teaching,* including English as a Second Language. *(Narrated in English. Remastered from the original 16mm films.)*

Children Learning Another Language: *An Innovative Approach*©

Color, 26 minutes, shows the excitement of children from K through 6th grades as they acquire **Spanish** and **French** with **TPR**. (ESL students will enjoy this too!)

If you are searching for ways that motivate children to learn another language, don't miss this classic video demonstration. The ideas you will see can be applied in your classroom for any grade level and for any language, including English as a second language.

Order Number **435-VHS** (Worldwide except PAL countries) • Order Number **435-DVD**

A Motivational Strategy for Language Learning©

Color, 25 minutes, demonstrates step-by-step how to apply **TPR** for best results with students between the ages of 17 and 60 acquiring **Spanish**. Easy to see how **TPR** can be used to teach any target language.

See the excitement on the faces of students as they understand everything the instructor is saying in Spanish. After several weeks in which the students are silent, but responding rapidly to commands in Spanish, students spontaneously begin to talk. You will see the amazing transition from understanding to speaking, reading, and writing!

Order Number **406-VHS** (Worldwide except PAL countries) • Order Number **406-DVD**

Strategy for Second Language Learning©

Color, 19 minutes, shows students from 17 to 60 acquiring **German** with **TPR**. Applies to <u>any</u> language!

Even when the class meets only two nights a week and no homework is required, the retention of spoken German is remarkable. You will be impressed by the graceful transition from understanding to speaking, reading, and writing!

Order Number **407-VHS** (Worldwide except PAL countries) • Order Number **407-DVD**

Demonstration of a New Strategy in Language Learning©

B&W, 15 minutes, shows American children acquiring **Japanese** with **TPR**. Applies to <u>any</u> language! You will see the first demonstration of the **Total Physical Response** ever recorded on film when American children rapidly internalize a complex sample of Japanese. You will also see the astonishing retention one year later! Narrated by the Originator of TPR, Dr. James J. Asher.

Order Number **408-VHS** (Worldwide except PAL countries) • Order Number **408-DVD**)

Captured for the first time on DVD!

The Northeastern Conference of FL/ESL instructors
Invited presentation by
Dr. James J. Asher

Narrated in English

Exciting TPR demonstration in Arabic and Spanish followed by a lively Q and A session.

Includes:

- How to stretch single words into hundreds of interesting sentences in any language.
- Your students will understand sentences, they have never heard before in the target language. This is the secret of fluency.
- Why it is <u>not</u> wise to tell your students, *"Listen and repeat after me!"*
- How to deal with adjectives.
- How to make the transition from understanding to speaking, reading and writing.
- How to deal with grammar.
- How to deal with abstractions.
- How to graduate your students with three or more languages.
- How to put your school on the map. Get ready for the Greyhound bus stopping at your school with teachers from around the world who want to take a look at your program.

Order Number: 104-DVD

Order from the catalog or directly from our website at: **www.tpr-world.com**
Recorded in 1992, re-mastered to digital and DVD in 2007.

A Second Language Classroom That Works!
Simple TPR Strategies that fill your classes with motivated students eager to learn!

New!   by award-winning language instructor,   Order # **98**
Joan Christopherson

For over 25 years, Ramiro Garcia has successfully applied the Total Physical Response in his high school and adult language classes.

This Triple-expanded Fourth Edition (over 300 pages) includes:

- ✓ Speaking, Reading, and Writing
- ✓ How to Create Your Own TPR Lessons.

And more than 200 TPR scenarios for beginning and advanced students.

- ✓ TPR Games for all age groups.
- ✓ TPR Testing for all skills including oral proficiency.

Instructor's Notebook: How to Apply TPR For Best Results
By **RAMIRO GARCIA**
Recipient of the **OUTSTANDING TEACHER AWARD**

In this illustrated book, Ramiro shares the tips and tricks that he has discovered in using TPR with hundreds of students. No matter what language you teach, including ESL and the sign language of the deaf, you will enjoy this insightful and humorous book.

Order #225

New! Just off the press! THE SEQUEL!!!

Instructor's Notebook: TPR Homework Exercises
by **RAMIRO GARCIA**
Recipient of the
MOST MEMORABLE TEACHER AWARD
and the
OUTSTANDING TEACHER AWARD
Edited by
James J. Asher

Ramiro's brand-new companion book to the Instructor's Notebook!

- ✓ Hundreds of TPR exercises your students can enjoy at home
- ✓ Catch-up exercises for students who have missed one or more classes.
- ✓ Review of the classroom TPR experience at home
- ✓ Helps other members of the student's family to acquire another language.
- ✓ Helps the teacher acquire the language of the students with exciting self-instructional exercises!

Order #224

The Graphics Book©

For Students of <u>All</u> Ages acquiring
English, Spanish, French, or German

by RAMIRO GARCIA

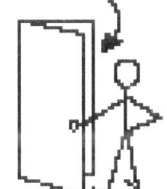

Dear Colleague;

You recall that I introduced graphics in the **Instructor's Notebook.** Hundreds of teachers discovered that **students of all ages** thoroughly enjoyed working with the material.

Your students understand a huge chunk of the target language because you used TPR. Now, with my new graphics book, you can follow up with **300 drawings** on tear-out strips that help your students zoom ahead with **more vocabulary, grammar, talking, reading** and **writing** in the target language.

You will receive **step-by-step guidance** in how to apply the graphics effectively with **children and adults** acquiring <u>any</u> language including **ESL**.

As an **extra bonus**, I provide you with **60 multiple-choice graphic tests for beginning and intermediate students.** Order in your choice of **English (#228)**, **Spanish (#229)**, **French (#236),** or **German (#237)**.

TPR BINGO© by Ramiro Garcia

In 25 years of applying the **Total Physical Response** in my high school and adult Spanish classes, **TPR Bingo** is the one game that students ask to play over and over!

When playing the game, students hear the instructor utter directions in the target language. As they advance in understanding, individual students ask to play the role of caller, which gives them valuable practice in **reading and speaking.** For an extra bonus, students **internalize numbers** in the target language from 1 through 100.

TPR Bingo comes with complete step-by-step directions for playing the game and rules for winning. There are 40 playboards (one side for beginners and the reverse side for advanced students). A master caller's board is included, with 100 pictures, chips, and caller-cards in your choice of **English (#226E)**, **Spanish (#226S)**, **French (#226F),** or **German (#226G)**. As I tell my colleagues, "Try this game with your students. You will love it—they will love it!"

Best wishes for continued success,

Ramiro Garcia

Brand-new feature! *Now included in every order of TPR Bingo...*

Play TPR Bingo with your students to move them from the imperative to the declarative (and interrogative). It's easy, it's fun, and you will love it!

A Language Classroom That Works for High-Speed Learning!

New!

by award-winning language instructor,
Joan Christopherson

Order # 98

Dear Colleague,

At my high school, we were disappointed that only 30 percent of the students enrolled in either Spanish or French, and then student interest faded after one or two years.

We were determined to transform our foreign language offering into an award-winning program, but how to do it? Well, after many years of trial and error, my colleagues and I developed some very simple TPR Strategies that worked beautifully!

Result: The demand for foreign languages exploded so much that our school added Russian, Italian, German and Japanese! A remarkable turnaround for any school.

Now I would like to share these TPR Strategies with you. They are quick and simple, and easily adapted to any grade level, any language, and any instructor's teaching style.

For all languages and all ages!

Sincerely,
Joan

e-mail: on_the_roaders@yahoo.com

PS: James Asher's TPR always starts with fast-moving comprehension of the target language in chunks rather than word-by-word.

Actionlogues
By **Jody Klopp**

✔ 25 happenings come to life in 396 photographs!
  Examples: Getting ready for work, making a sandwich, going on a date, driving a car, etc.

✔ Internalize 160 verbs.

✔ Native speaker on a cassette utters each direction in the target language. Listen and understand instantly by looking at a photo.

✔ **Added Bonus:** Great way for non-native language teachers to expand vocabulary.

More LIVE ACTION
in English, Spanish, French, or German!

Order #	Title:	Price
245	Actionlogues **Booklet** in **English**	
246	Actionlogues **Audio Cassette - English**	
230	Actionlogues **Booklet** in **Spanish**	
231	Actionlogues **Audio Cassette - Spanish**	
232	Actionlogues **Booklet** in **French**	
233	Actionlogues **Audio Cassette - French**	
234	Actionlogues **Booklet** in **German**	
235	Actionlogues **Audio Cassette - German**	

TPR IS MORE THAN COMMANDS —*AT ALL LEVELS*

CONTEE SEELY & ELIZABETH ROMIJN
Winner of the Excellence in Teaching Award

Explodes myths about the Total Physical Response:
  Myth 1: TPR is limited to commands.
  Myth 2: TPR is only useful at the beginning of language acquisition.

Demonstrates how you can use Professor James Asher's approach—

✔ to *overcome problems* typically encountered in the use of TPR,

✔ to teach *tenses* and *verb forms* in *any language* in 6 ways,

✔ to teach *grammar, idioms*, and *fluent discourse* in a natural way, and

✔ to help your students *tell stories* that move them into fluent speaking, reading, and writing.

Shows you how to go from zero to correct spoken fluency with TPR.

Order #	Title:	Price
95	TPR is More Than Commands All All Levels	

TPR for Students of All Ages!

For 30 years, "Listen & Perform" worked for students of all ages learning English in the Amazon - and it will work for your students too!

Order this popular Student Book in your choice of **ENGLISH**, **SPANISH** or **FRENCH**!

Your students in elementary and middle school will enjoy more than 150 exciting pages of stimulating right brain **Total Physical Response** exercises such as:

drawing • *pointing* • *touching* • *matching* • *moving people, places, and things*

With the **Student Book** and companion **Cassette**, each of your students can perform <u>alone at their desks</u> or <u>at home</u> to advance from comprehension to sophisticated skills of speaking, reading, and writing! These books by **Stephen M. Silvers** are chock-full of fun and productive TPR activities!

Order #	Title:	Recommendation:
271	Teacher's Guidebook for All Languages (in **English**)	TPR Lessons for children in elementary and middle school. Order in English, Spanish, or French! (Packed with fun activities for older students too!)
270	Listen and Perform **Student Book** in **English**	
272	Listen and Perform **Audio Cassette** in **English**	
209E	Special 3 in 1 - Teacher's, Student Book, & Cassette (**English**)	
274	Listen and Perform **Student Book** in **Spanish**	
276	Listen and Perform **Audio Cassette** in **Spanish**	
209S	Special 3 in 1 - Teacher's, Student Book, & Cassette (**Spanish**)	
275	Listen and Perform **Student Book** in **French**	
277	Listen and Perform **Audio Cassette** in **French**	
209F	Special 3 in 1 - Teacher's, Student Book, & Cassette (**French**)	

TPR for Young Children!

- Marvelously **simple format:** Glance at a page and instantly move your students in a logical series of actions.
- **Initial screening test** tells you each student's skill.
- After each lesson, there is a **competency test** for each students.
- Recommended for **preschool**, **kindergarden**, and **elementary**.

Order #	Title:
240	**Learning With Movements - English**
241	**Learning With Movements - Spanish**
242	**Learning With Movements - French**

How to TPR Grammar

For Beginning, Intermediate, and Advanced Students of All Ages!

Edited by William Denevan, Trainer of Foreign Language Teachers at Stanford University.

"TPR is fine for commands, but how can I use it with other grammatical features?"

Eric Schessler shows you how to apply **TPR** for <u>stress-free</u> <u>acquisition</u> of <u>50</u> <u>grammatical</u> <u>features</u> such as:

Abstract Nouns	Expletives	Past Continuous	Prepositions of Place	Singular/Plural Nouns
Adjectives	Future - to be going to	Past Perfect	Prepositions of Time	Subject Pronouns
Adverbs	Future - Will	Past tense of **Be**	Present Continuous	Tag Questions
Articles	Have - Present and Past	Possessive Case	Present Perfect	Verbs
Conjunctions	Interrogative Verb forms	and **Of** expressions	Simple Past	Wh - Questions
Demonstratives	Manipulatives	Possessive Pronouns	Simple Present	
	Object Pronouns			

Order #	Title:		Recommendation:
260	**English Grammar Through Actions**	by Eric Schessler	**ESL Students of All Ages**
261	**Spanish Grammar Through Actions**	by Eric Schessler	**Students of Spanish of All Ages**
262	**French Grammar Through Actions**	by Eric Schessler	**Students of French of All Ages**

Look, I Can Talk!
Original Student Book for Level 1
in English, Spanish, French or German

Editor's Tip...
For best results, TPR the concrete words that will appear in the story!

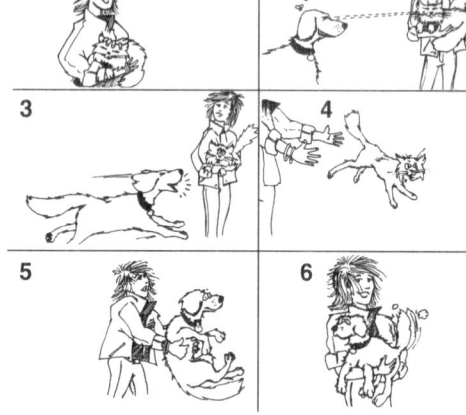

Step-by-step, Blaine Ray shows you how to tell a story with **physical actions**, then have your students *tell the story to each other* in their own words **using the target language**, then **act** it out, **write** it and **read** it. Each **Student Book for Level 1** comes in your choice of *English, Spanish, French* or *German* and has

- ✔ 12 main stories
- ✔ 24 additional action-packed picture stories
- ✔ Many options for retelling each story
- ✔ Reading and writing exercises galore.

Blaine _personally guarantees_ that each of your students will eagerly tell stories in the target language by using the **Student Book**.

Follow the steps in the **Teacher's Guidebook** and then work story-by-story with easy-to-use **Overhead Transparencies**.

Order #	Title:	
110	Look, I Can Talk!	*Teacher's Guidebook for All Languages* (In English)
115	Look, I Can Talk!	*Student Book for Level 1* - **English**
116	Look, I Can Talk!	*Student Book for Level 1* - **Spanish**
117	Look, I Can Talk!	*Student Book for Level 1* - **French**
118	Look, I Can Talk!	*Student Book for Level 1* - **German**
111	Look, I Can Talk!	*Overhead Transparencies for All Languages*

This is the original book that started TPRS!

Look, I Can Talk _More_!
Student Book for Level 2
by Blaine Ray with Joe Neilson, Dave Cline, Carole Stevens, and Christopher Taleck

Once again Blaine uses his exciting technique of blending **physical actions** with interesting story lines to get the students **talking**, **reading**, and **writing** in the **target language**. This second series of stories continues to build vocabulary while focusing on more advanced grammatical concepts common to second year language classes (i.e., use of infinitives, reflexive verbs, direct and indirect object pronouns, preterite vs. imperfect, etc.) Students enjoy using the target language to describe the stories as well as stories they have created.

Order #	Title::		
120	Look, I Can Talk _More_!	Student Book for Level 2 - **English**	**Level 2 ESL Students**
122	Look, I Can Talk _More_!	Student Book for Level 2 - **Spanish**	**Level 2 Spanish Students**
123	Look, I Can Talk _More_!	Student Book for Level 2 - **French**	**Level 2 French Students**
121	Look, I Can Talk _More_!	Student Book for Level 2 - **German**	**Level 2 German Students**
124	Look, I Can Talk _More_!	Overhead Transparencies for All Languages	**To help you demonstrate 10 main stories**

Look, I'm _Still_ Talking!
Student Book for Level 3

Order #	Title:		
125	Look, I'm _Still_ Talking!	Student Book for Level 3 - **English**	**Level 3 ESL Students**
126	Look, I'm _Still_ Talking!	plus *Mini-stories* - **Spanish**	**Level 3 Spanish Students**
127	Look, I'm _Still_ Talking!	Student Book for Level 3 - **French**	**Level 3 French Students**
128	Look, I'm _Still_ Talking!	Student Book for Level 3 - **German**	**Level 3 German Students**
724	Look, I'm _Still_ Talking!	Overhead Transparencies for All Languages	**To help you demonstrate the main stories**

Fluency Thru TPR Storytelling
by Blaine Ray and Contee Seely

How to use storytelling for best results at any level. Frequently Asked Questions, and much, much more!

Order #	Title:	
96	Fluency Thru TPR Storytelling	**Works with all languages**

Look, I Can Talk Extras

Order Number | Title | Price

Spanish Mini-Novels

- 901 Pobre Ana - Blaine Ray (Spanish mini-novel)
- 902 Casi se muere - Lisa Ray Turner y Blaine Ray (Spanish mini-novel)
- 903 El viaje de su vida - Lisa Ray Turner y Blaine Ray (Spanish mini-novel)
- 904 ¡Viva el toro! (Spanish mini-novel)
- 906 Patricia va a California (Spanish mini-novel)
- 908 ¿Dónde está Eduardo? (Spanish mini-novel)
- 909 Mi propio auto (Spanish mini-novel)
- 900 El viaje perdido (Spanish mini-novel)

French Mini-Novels

- 905 Pauvre Anne (French mini-novel)
- 919 Presque Mort (French mini-novel)
- 920 Le voyage de sa vie (French mini-novel)
- 921 Fama va en Californie (French mini-novel)
- 922 Vive le taureau (French mini-novel)
- 923 Le Voyage perdu (French mini-novel)

German Mini-Novels

- 924 Petra reist nach Kalifornien (German mini-novel)
- 930 Arme Anna (German mini-novel)

Editor's Tip...
If you TPR the vocabulary first, your students will be thrilled that they understand the story the first time they read it.

How to TPR Vocabulary!

For long-term retention, be sure to TPR the words <u>before</u> you tell a story. *The Command Book* shows you how to TPR most of the words in Blaine Ray's *Look I Can Talk* series and Todd McKay's *TPR Storytelling* series.

- Giant 300 page resource book, alphabetized for quick look-up.
- Yes, includes *abstractions!*
- As a bonus, you will discover how to TPR 2,000 vocabulary items from traditional Level 1 and Level 2 textbooks.

Look up the word... **How to TPR it**
Where 1. Pedro, stand up and run to the door. Maria, sit **where** Pedro was sitting.
2. Write the name of the country **where** you were born. 3. Touch a student who's from a country **where** the people speak Spanish (French, English).

Order #	Title:	Recommendation:
273	The Command Book	All Languages and All Ages

The **Command Book**
How to TPR 2,000 Vocabulary Items in Any Language
by STEPHEN SILVERS

TPR Storytelling

by

Todd McKay

- ✔ Pre-tested in the classroom for 8 years to guarantee success for your students.
- ✔ Easy to follow, step-by-step guidance each day for three school years - one year at a time.
- ✔ Todd shows you how to switch from activity to activity to keep the novelty alive for your students day after day.
- ✔ Evidence shows the approach works: Students in storytelling class outperformed students in the traditional ALM class.
- ✔ Each story comes illustrated with snazzy cartoons that appeal to students of all ages.
- ✔ There is continuity to the story line because the stories revolve around one family.
- ✔ Complete with tests to assess comprehension, speaking, reading and writing.
- ✔ Yes, cultural topics are included.
- ✔ Yes, stories include most of the content you will find in traditional textbooks including vocabulary and grammar.
- ✔ Yes, included is a brief refresher of classic TPR, by the originator—
  Dr. James J. Asher.
- ✔ Yes, games are included.
- ✔ Yes, your students will have the long-term retention you expect from TPR instructions.
- ✔ Yes, Todd includes his e-mail address to answer your questions if you get stuck along the way.
- ✔ Yes, you can order a video demonstration showing you step-by-step how to apply every feature in the Teacher's Guidebook.

Order Number	Title
400	Student Book - Year 1 **English**
401	Student Book - Year 2 **English**
402	Student Book - Year 3 **English**
410	Student Book - Year 1 **Spanish**
411	Student Book - Year 2 **Spanish**
412	Student Book - Year 3 **Spanish**
420	Student Book - Year 1 **French**
421	Student Book - Year 2 **French**
422	Student Book - Year 3 **French**
430	Complete Testing Packet for **English** Listening, Reading, Speaking, and Writing
431	Complete Testing Packet for **Spanish** Listening, Reading, Speaking, and Writing
432	Complete Testing Packet for **French** Listening, Reading, Speaking, and Writing
440	Teacher's Guidebook for **English**
441	Teacher's Guidebook for **Spanish**
442	Teacher's Guidebook for **French** .
450	Transparencies for All Languages - Year 1
451	Transparencies for All Languages - Year 2
452	Transparencies for All Languages - Year 3
460	TPR Storytelling Video *Shows every step in the Teacher's Guidebook.*

Sky Oaks Productions, Inc.
P.O. Box 1102 • Los Gatos, CA, USA 95031
Phone: (408) 395-7600 • Fax: (408) 395-8440
e-mail: tprworld@aol.com
www.tpr—world.com
California residents: add sales tax. Prices subject to change without notice.

Use your VISA, MasterCard, or Discover Card to order from anywhere in the world!
WE SHIP ASAP!   FREE TPR Catalog upon request!

Exciting new products from Todd McKay!
TPR Index Cards
(Easy-to-handle 4x5 cards)

1. Index cards tell you exactly what to say, lesson by lesson.
2. 60 Cards with vocabulary from First Year textbooks.
3. When your students internalize this vocabulary, they're ready for a smooth transition to stories.
4. No need to fumble through a book.
5. No need to make up your own lessons.
6. Quick! Easy to use! Classroom-tested for success!
7. Works for students of all ages, including adults!

470	TPR Index Cards for **English**
471	TPR Index Cards for **Spanish**
472	TPR Index Cards for **French**
473	TPR Index Cards for **German**

Dear Colleague:

I want to share with you the **TPR Lessons** that my high school and college students have **thoroughly enjoyed** and **retained** for weeks—even months later. My book has...

- A script you may follow step-by-step including a list of props needed to conduct each class.
- A command format that students thoroughly enjoy. (Students show their understanding of the spoken language by successfully carrying out the commands given to them by the instructor. **Production** is delayed until students are ready and feel comfortable.)
- Grammar taught implicitly through the imperative.
- Tests for an evaluation of student achievement.

Sincerely,

Francisco Cabello, Ph.D.

TOTAL PHYSICAL RESPONSE IN THE FIRST YEAR

By **FRANCISCO L. CABELLO** with William Denevan

Order #	Title:
221	Total Physical Response in First Year English
220	Total Physical Response in First Year Spanish
222	Total Physical Response in First Year French

Recommendation:

TPR Lessons for high school, college, and adults.

LIVE ACTION
English, Spanish, French, German, Italian, or Japanese!!

Each page is a "happening" — a list of imperatives to be performed in the classroom with props. There are 67 happenings such as Washing Your Hands, Going Swimming, Using a Pay Phone, Taking Pictures, and Going to the Movies (Go to the movie theater. Buy a ticket. Give it to the ticket-taker at the door, etc.)

Excellent for all levels. Basic survival vocabulary can be used as a basis for a great variety of lessons, especially verb work.

Elizabeth Romijn and Contee Seely

Order #	Title:
255	Live Action **English**
227	Live Action **English** - Audio Cassettes
256	Live Action **Spanish**
257	Live Action **French**
258	Live Action **German**
259	Live Action **Italian**
226	Live Action **Japanese**

Prize-Winning!
COMPREHENSION BASED LANGUAGE LESSONS
by Margaret S. Woodruff, Ph.D.

Here are **detailed lesson plans** for **60 hours** of TPR Instruction that make it **easy** for novice instructors to apply the **total physical response** approach **at any level**. The **TPR lessons** include

- **Step-by-step directions** so that instructors **in any foreign language** (including ESL) can apply comprehension training successfully.
- **Competency tests** to be given after the 10th and 30th lessons.
- **Pretested short exercises**—dozens of them to capture student interest.
- **Many photographs**

NOTE!
We have printed the lessons in two languages — **English** and **German**, but we have charged you only the cost of printing a single language.

Winner of the Paul Pimsleur Award
(With Dr. Janet King Swaffar)

Order #	Title:
290-P	Comprehension Based Language Lessons - Level 1

Laura J. Ayala

FAVORITE GAMES FOR FL - ESL CLASSES

(For All Levels and All Languages)
by
Laura Ayala & Dr. Margaret Woodruff-Wieding

Order #291

Chapter 1: Introduction

Chapter 2: Getting Started with Games
- How to get students involved
- How the games were selected or invented.

Chapter 3: Game Learning Categories
- Alphabet and Spelling
- Changing Case
- Changing Tense
- Changing Voice
- Describing Actions
- Describing Objects

Chapter 3 (Cont.)
- Getting Acquainted
- Giving Commands
- Hearing and Pronouncing
- Statements & Questions
- Negating Sentences
- Numbers and Counting
- Parts of the Body and Grooming
- Plurals and Telling How Many
- Possessive Adjectives & Belonging
- Recognizing Related Words
- Telling Time
- Using Correct Word Order.

Chapter 4: Games by Technique
- Responding to Commands
- Guessing
- Simulating
- Listing
- Categorizing
- Associating
- Sequencing
- Matching

Chapter 5: Special Materials For Games
- Objects
- Authentic Props
- Pictures
- Cards
- Stories

Chapter 6: Bibliography

✓ FIND the products you want from our TPR Catalog.
✓ WRITE on this Order Form or your School Purchase Order the items you want.
✓ FAX or MAIL the Order Form and/or School Purchase Order to us. We'll do the rest, pronto!

TPR ORDER FORM
BOOKS • VIDEO DEMONSTRATIONS • STUDENT KITS • GAMES

Sky Oaks Productions, Inc.
P.O. Box 1102 • Los Gatos, California, USA 95031
Since 1973

Phone: (408) 395-7600
e-mail: tprworld@aol.com
Fax: (408) 395-8440

Use your VISA, Discover, or MasterCard to order from anywhere in the world! WE SHIP ASAP!

Please Print or Type:

Name _____ Date of Order: _____

School or Residence _____

Street or P.O. Box _____ City _____ State _____ Zip _____

Country _____ Phone (___) _____ Fax (___) _____ E-mail _____
Please print.

Discover Card, Visa/MC Card No. ☐☐☐☐ ☐☐☐☐ ☐☐☐☐ ☐☐☐☐

EXPIRATION DATE _____ Authorized Signature _____

PAGE	ORDER NO.	QUANTITY	DESCRIPTION & LANGUAGE	EACH	TOTAL

☐ Send **order form** only
☐ Send **complete catalog** plus **complimentary article**
☐ My **Check** or **Purchase Order** is enclosed.

Subtotal

California residents: Add sales tax

USA: Add 12% for shipping & handling (minimum: $5.95)

Outside USA: for S & H **add 30%** (minimum: $10.95)

P.S. To order **directly online**, visit our website at: **www.tpr-world.com**

Prices subject to change without notice.

(U.S. Currency) Total $_____

Order Form

TPR PRODUCTS

**Books • Games
Student Kits
Teacher Kits
Audio Cassettes
Video Demonstrations**

Order directly from the publisher using your
<u>VISA</u>, <u>MASTERCARD</u>, *or* <u>DISCOVER CARD</u>
WE SHIP ASAP TO ANYWHERE IN THE WORLD!

Sky Oaks Productions, Inc.
TPR World Headquarters Since 1973
P.O. Box 1102
Los Gatos, CA 95031 USA

Phone: (408) 395-7600
Fax: (408) 395-8440
E-mail: tprworld@aol.com

FREE CATALOG UPON REQUEST!

 *For fast service,
order online by clicking on:*
www.tpr-world.com